JUST DESSERTS

A collection of delicious easy-to-make recipes

GW00402177

Contents

Originally published in 2010 by L&K Designs. This edition published in 2010 by Myriad Books Limited
© L&K Designs 2010
PRINTED IN CHINA

Publishers Disclaimer

Whilst every effort has been made to ensure that the information contained is correct, the publisher cannot be held responsible for any errors and or omissions. Please note certain recipes may contain nuts or nut oil.

Desserts

When you fancy something a little naughty but nice ...and whether you call it sweet, pudding or afters, the end to a meal is the part we often look forward to most.

Packed with delicious mouth-watering recipes to inspire you, from puddings to pies, meringues to mousses, crumbles to cakes and sorbets to syllabubs.

With easy-to-follow recipes, including quick and simple every day desserts through to the comfort foods of days gone by; with elaborate recipes for special occasions - covering the traditional and not so traditional, let us help you fall in love with desserts all over again!

Apple Pie (Serves 4)

Ingredients

350g/12oz plain flour
pinch of salt
150g/6oz butter
1 tbsp caster sugar
1 egg, lightly beaten
700g/1 1/2 lb cooking apples
juice of 1/2 lemon
100g/4oz sultanas
75g/3oz soft light brown sugar
pinch of ground cinnamon
pinch of freshly grated nutmeg
grated rind and juice of 1 orange
milk, to glaze
caster sugar for sprinkling

Method

1. To make the pastry, put the flour and salt in a bowl and rub in the butter until the mixture resembles fine breadcrumbs. Stir in the caster sugar, then stir in the egg and enough water to bind the mixture together.

2. Knead lightly on a lightly floured surface, then roll out two-thirds of the pastry and use to line a shallow pie dish. Peel, core and thinly slice the apples. Put in a bowl and sprinkle with lemon juice.

3. Layer the apples, sultanas, brown sugar, spices and orange rind in the pie dish. Sprinkle with the orange juice. Roll out the remaining pastry to form a lid, pressing the edges together. Scallop the edges, then make a slit in the centre of the pie.

4. Brush the top with milk to glaze, then bake at 200C/400F/Gas Mark 6 for 30 minutes, until golden brown. Sprinkle the top with caster sugar and serve hot or cold. Accompany with dairy ice cream.

Apple Turnover Tart (Serves 6-8)

Ingredients

175g/6oz wholemeal flour
pinch of salt
1 tsp ground cinnamon
100g/4oz caster (superfine) sugar
225g/8oz unsalted (sweet) butter
cold water, to mix
1kg cooking (tart) apples, sliced
50g/2oz light brown sugar
3 tbsps icing (confectioners') sugar

Method

1. Put the flour, salt and cinnamon in a bowl. Add 2 tbsps of the caster sugar. Dice 100g/4oz of the butter and rub in with the fingertips until the mixture resembles fine breadcrumbs.

2. Mix with enough cold water to form a firm dough. Wrap in clingfilm (plastic wrap) and chill for 30 minutes.

3. Melt 75g/3oz of the remaining butter in a pan. Remove from the heat and add the apple slices and remaining caster sugar. Toss thoroughly. Grease a 23cm/9in deep round pie dish with the remaining butter. Add the apple mixture in layers with the brown sugar.

4. Roll out the pastry to a round and use to cover the pie dish. Trim. Make several slits to allow steam to escape. Bake in a preheated oven at 190C/370F/Gas Mark 5 for about 1 hour or until the apple is tender and the pastry is golden brown.

5. Carefully turn out the tart on to a serving plate. Sprinkle liberally with the icing sugar and flash under a hot grill (broiler) for 3 minutes to caramelize.

Baked Apples (Serves 6-8)
Ingredients

6-8 medium to large apples (cored)
3 clementine oranges (peeled, sectioned & chopped)
75g/1/2 cup of golden raisins
2-3 tsps cinnamon
1/4 cup of cold water
75g/1 cup of pecan nuts (optional)

Method

1. Place the chopped orange sections, raisins and cinnamon in a bowl and mix together. Stuff the cored apples with fruit and place in the slow cooker.

2. Add the cold water, (to surround the apples), cover and cook on a low temperature for 7 to 8 hours. Remove from cooker and add pecans for decoration.

Bakewell Tart (Serves 8)
Ingredients for Pastry

170g/1 1/2 cups plain flour
pinch of salt
75g/1/2 cup unsalted butter

Ingredients for filling and topping

170g strawberry or raspberry jam
110g unsalted butter
110g vanilla sugar
110g ground almonds,
3 eggs, plus one additional egg yolk
1 tsp almond extract
handful blanched flaked almonds

Method

1. Combine the flour and salt in a large bowl. Rub in the butter until the mixture resembles fine breadcrumbs.

2. Stir in enough iced water to bring the mixture together into a smooth dough. Roll the pastry out to line a 23cm tart tin and chill for 30 minutes, or until required.

Bakewell Tart/cont.

3. Preheat the oven to 200C/400F/Gas Mark 6. Spread a layer of jam generously over the tart base.

4. Melt the butter and continue to heat until it smells nutty. Whisk together the sugar, ground almonds, egg yolks, egg whites and almond extract. Pour in the hot butter and whisk until smooth. Spoon the mixture over the jam.

5. Transfer the tart to the oven and bake for about 30 minutes, until lightly browned and just set, scattering the flaked almonds over the tart after 25 minutes so that they get a chance to brown slightly. Remove from the oven and leave to cool for about 20 minutes.

Baklavas (Serves 6)

Ingredients

5 whole cloves
1 tsp ground cinnamon
1 cinnamon stick
2 tbsps clear honey
225g/1 1/2 cups of mixed nuts (chopped)
75g/1/3 cup of butter (unsalted)
12 sheets of filo pastry (all buttered)
170g/3/4 cup of dark brown sugar
150ml/2/3 cup of water

Method

1. Preheat the oven to 190C/375F/Gas Mark 5. Grease a Swiss roll tin with butter. Take 4 sheets of the filo pastry and layer the base of the tin.

2. Place the sugar, nuts and cinnamon in a bowl and mix together. Sprinkle half of the mixture over the pastry in the tin. Layer over the top with another 4 sheets of filo pastry and cover with the other half of the sugar/nuts mixture.

3. Layer the final 4 sheets of filo pastry over the top. Cut the edges, where needed, and cut the pastry into the required number of rectangles. Place in the oven and cook for 25-30 minutes, until lightly browned. Remove from the oven and allow to cool for a couple of minutes.

4. Place the remaining sugar in a saucepan with the clear honey, cloves and cinnamon stick. Add the water and bring to the boil. Reduce the heat and simmer for 8-10 minutes. Pour the spiced mixture over the still-warm baklavas and leave to cool for 5-10 minutes.

Bread & Butter Pudding (Serves 4-6)

Ingredients

115g/3/4 cup of sultanas
8 tbsps orange marmalade (thick-cut)
7-8 slices white bread (crusts removed)
55g/1/4 cup of butter (softened)
225ml/1 cup of double cream
225ml/1 cup of milk
3 eggs
55g/1/4 cup of caster sugar
1/2 tsp vanilla essence
icing sugar (for dusting)

Method

1. Preheat the oven to 190C/375F/Gas Mark 5. Lightly butter a shallow ovenproof dish. Spread butter on one side of each slice of bread, then spread with marmalade. Put the bread, marmalade side-up, in the base of the ovenproof dish. Cut any remaining bread into triangles.

2. Sprinkle the marmalade bread with sultanas and then arrange the bread triangles over the top. Place the milk, eggs, caster sugar and double cream in a bowl and whisk together well. Stir in the vanilla essence.

3. Push through a sieve into a pouring jug and pour over the bread mixture in the dish. Leave to soak for 3-5 minutes. Place the dish inside a large roasting tin and pour in hot water, until it reaches halfway up the sides of the dish.

4. Place in the oven for 25-30 minutes, until the top is golden brown and the custard is setting, but not firm. Remove from the oven and leave to cool for 10 minutes. Dust with icing sugar. Preheat the grill to a medium setting and place under the grill for 1-2 minutes, until golden. Serve with vanilla ice cream or whipped cream.

Cherry Pie (Serves 4)

Ingredients

300g plain flour, plus extra for dusting
150g chilled unsalted butter, cubed, plus extra for greasing
100g golden caster sugar
1 large egg yolk
1 tbsp cornflour
pinch of ground cinnamon
500g cherries (stoned)
1 tbsp milk (for brushing)
2 tbsps golden granulated sugar

Method

1. Put the flour, butter and 75g of the golden caster sugar into a food processor and pulse until the mixture resembles crumbs. Add the egg yolk and 2-3 tablespoons cold water. Pulse until the mixture comes together to form a ball. Turn out, wrap in cling film and chill for 30 minutes.

2. Mix the cornflour, remaining golden caster sugar and cinnamon together, then gently toss with the cherries in a bowl. Put a baking sheet into the oven and preheat to 220C/450F/Gas Mark 7.

3. Grease a 23cm pie dish – ideally one made of enamel or metal. Roll out half the pastry onto a lightly floured surface and use to line the dish. Trim the edges, pile the cherry mixture into the centre and spoon over 4 tablespoons water.

4. Brush the pastry edges with water. Roll out the remaining pastry and use to cover the fruit, making a hole in the centre. Press the edges to seal, trim off the excess pastry and crimp the edges with your forefinger and thumb.

5. Brush the pie with milk and sprinkle with the granulated sugar. Put the pie on the baking sheet in the oven and bake for 15 minutes. Reduce the oven temperature to 180C/350F/Gas Mark 4 and bake for a further 15-20 minutes until the pastry is pale-golden.

Chocolate Pudding (Serves 4)

Ingredients

50g/1 cup of soft breadcrumbs (from bread)
175g/1 cup of dark chocolate (broken into pieces)
110ml/1/2 cup of milk
110ml/1/2 cup of condensed milk
2 tbsps butter (softened)
1 tbsp caster sugar
1/2 tsp vanilla essence

Method

1. This is a recipe for cooking in a pressure cooker. Grease a 6in tin mould with butter. Place the chocolate and milk in a saucepan and melt the chocolate over a low heat, stirring continuously.

2. Remove from the heat and stir in the breadcrumbs; combine well. Set to one side. Place the butter and sugar in a large mixing bowl and cream together until light and fluffy.

3. Add the vanilla essence, condensed milk and chocolate mixture and mix together well.

4. Transfer the mixture into the pudding tin mould and cover with foil. Place in the pressure cooker and cook for 2 whistles.

5. Allow any steam to disperse before opening. Turn out onto a serving plate and serve hot with custard or ice-cream.

Custard Tart (Serves 6-8)

Ingredients

225g/8oz plain shortcrust pastry
600ml/1 pint single cream
pared rind of 1/2 lemon
1 vanilla pod split lengthways
strand of saffron
3 eggs, plus 2 extra egg yolks (lightly beaten)
55g/2oz golden caster sugar
1 1/2 whole nutmegs (freshly grated)
1 tbsp butter for dotting on the top

Method

1. Line a deep 23cm (9in) tart tin with the pastry and pre-bake or bake blind. Pre-heat the oven to 180C/350F/Gas Mark 4 and place a baking tray inside to pre-heat.

2. Put the cream in a saucepan with the lemon rind, vanilla pod and saffron and leave to stand for 5 minutes. Gently heat the cream mixture until almost boiling, then remove the pan from the heat.

3. Meanwhile, whisk the eggs, egg yolks and sugar together in a large heatproof jug, but without producing any frothy bubbles.

4. Pour the cream through a strainer on to the egg mixture, together with half the grated nutmeg and vanilla essence (if not using a vanilla pod). Stir up again to mix well and to make sure the eggs are not just sitting at the bottom of the jug.

5. Place the pre-baked pastry case on the hot baking tray and then fill the pastry case with the custard mixture - do this carefully to avoid flooding. Sprinkle more nutmeg on top and dot with the butter.

6. Carefully replace the baking tray in the centre of the oven and bake for 30 - 40 minutes or until golden brown, speckled and slightly risen up in the centre.

Gooseberry Fool (Serves 4)

Ingredients

350g gooseberries
1 tbsp water
75g caster sugar (or to taste)
284ml carton double cream
200g cold, ready-made, fresh custard

Method

1. Put the gooseberries in a saucepan with the water and place over a medium heat. Bring to a simmer and cook for 5-10 minutes or until the gooseberries are very soft, squashing them with a spoon as they cook.

2. Purée in a blender then press through a sieve to remove the pips. Stir the sugar into the sieved purée, adding more if the fruit is very tart, then leave to cool completely.

3. Whip the cream until it holds soft peaks, then fold it loosely into the custard. Loosely fold in the gooseberry purée so the fool has a marbled texture. Serve chilled, in small glasses.

Jam Roly Poly (Serves 6)

Ingredients

250g/8oz self-raising flour
125g/4oz shredded suet
90-120ml/6-8 tablespoons water
4 tablespoons raspberry jam
pinch of salt
1 egg, beaten, and caster sugar to glaze

Method

1. Preheat your oven to 200C/400F/Gas Mark 6. Grease and flour a 23 x 33cm baking sheet. Over a medium heat, gently warm the jam in a saucepan but do not allow to boil.

2. Sift the flour into a bowl with the salt then add the suet and just enough water to create a soft dough. Do not add too much water - the dough should not be sticky.

Jam Roly Poly/cont.

3. On a floured surface roll the dough into a rectangle about 20x30cm. Brush the dough with the warmed jam, but leave a border of about 1cm. Fold in this border and brush with milk.

4. With the shorter side towards you, roll the pastry loosely. Once the roll is complete seal the edge, again by brushing with a little milk. Put the roll on the greased baking sheet, with the sealed edge underneath. Brush with the beaten egg and sprinkle with caster sugar. Bake for 35-40 minutes until golden brown then serve hot with custard.

Key Lime Pie (Serves 2)
Ingredients

75g/3oz butter
225g/8oz digestive biscuits, crushed
300ml/1/2 pint double cream
juice and rind of 4 large limes
220ml/1 cup condensed milk
whipped cream and lime slices (to decorate)

Method

1. Melt the butter, stir in the crushed biscuits. Press into the base and sides of a 20.5cm (8in) deep, loose-bottomed, fluted flan tin. Chill.

2. For the filling, whisk together the remaining ingredients until thick and creamy. Spoon over the biscuit base. Chill, then just before serving, pipe the whipped cream around the edge of the pie and decorate with the lime slices.

Kulfi (Serves 4-6)

Ingredients

620ml/2 3/4 cups of creamy milk
450ml/2 cups of double cream
2 tbsps honey
50g/2/3 cup of almonds (chopped)
25g/1/4 cup of pistachio nuts (chopped)
3 cardamom pods

Method

1. Pour the milk in a saucepan and add the cardamom pods. Bring just to the boil and reduce the heat. Simmer until reduced by about 150ml.

2. Reduce to a gentle heat and stir in the cream. Continue to heat, stirring continuously, until the mixture has reduced to about 600ml. Remove from the heat.

3. Remove the cardamom pods and stir in the almonds, honey and half of the pistachio nuts. Leave to cool completely.

4. Transfer to a freezer-safe container and freeze for 1-2 hours. Stir the mixture and then return to the freezer for 7-8 hours, until firm.

5. Remove from the freezer for 20-30 minutes to soften a little prior to serving. Serve with a sprinkling of the remaining pistachios.

Lemon Meringue Pie (Serves 6)

Ingredients

110ml/1/2 cup of lemon juice
1 tbsp grated lemon zest
1 pre-prepared pie crust
5 egg yolks (slightly beaten)
5 egg whites
450ml/2 cups of water
110g/1/2 cup of caster sugar
1/2 tsp cream of tartar
75g/1/2 cup of cornstarch
2 tbsps butter
1/8 tsp salt

Method

1. Preheat the oven to 180C/350F/Gas Mark 4.

2. Place the sugar, cornstarch and salt in a pan and mix together. Gradually add the water, stirring continuously. Place over a medium heat and bring to the boil and boil for 1 minute.

3. Stir half of the mixture into the egg yolks, mixing gently. Once mixed, stir this mixture into the water mixture in the pan.

4. Remove the pan from the heat and add the lemon juice, lemon zest and butter. Leave to cool a little for 4-5 minutes, then pour into the pie crust.

5. Place the egg whites and cream of tartar in a bowl and beat together with an electric whisk, until frothy. Gradually add the caster sugar and keep beating the mixture until it forms hard peaks.

6. Spread the meringue mixture evenly over the top of the pie with a spoon – do not leave any gaps.

7. Place in the oven and bake for 20-25 minutes, until the meringue is golden and crispy and the underneath is of a marshmallow-like consistency.

Peach Melba & Ice-Cream (Serves 4)

Ingredients

4 scoops of vanilla ice-cream
2 ripe peaches (halved & stoned)
125g/1 cup of raspberries
25g/1/3 cup of almonds (slivered)
30g/1/8 cup of sugar
1 1/2 tbsps icing sugar
150ml/2/3 cup of water
1 tbsp butter

Method

1. Place the sugar and water in a pan and bring to the boil. Reduce the heat and simmer for 4-5 minutes. Add the peach halves and simmer for 8-10 minutes, until tender.

2. Remove the peaches from the water with a slotted spoon and leave to cool. Place the icing sugar and raspberries in a food processor and blend until smooth. Press the contents through a sieve into a small bowl and place in the refrigerator to chill.

3. Heat the butter in a frying pan and add the almonds. Cook gently for a couple of minutes, until golden brown. Remove with a slotted spoon and drain any fat on paper kitchen towel.

4. Peel the peach halves, (the outer peel should come off easily). Arrange between two serving dishes and add a scoop of ice-cream.

5. Pour over the chilled raspberry sauce and sprinkle the almonds over the top. Serve immediately.

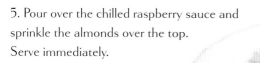

Pecan Pie (Serves 4-6)

Ingredients

350g/12oz puff pastry (paste), thawed if frozen
150g/5oz pecan halves
75g/3oz butter
175g/6oz light brown sugar
4 eggs
4 tbsps golden (light corn) syrup
2 tbsps boiling water
1 tsp vanilla essence (extract)

Method

1. Roll out the pastry and use to line a 20cm/8in flan dish (pie pan) on a baking (cookie) sheet. Reserve 25g of the nuts for decoration and roughly chop the remainder.

2. Beat the butter and sugar until fluffy. Beat in the eggs one at a time, beating well after each addition. Mix the syrup with the boiling water and stir in with the nuts and vanilla essence.

3. Turn into the pastry case (pie shell) and bake in a preheated oven at 200C/400F/Gas Mark 6 for 15 minutes. Remove from the oven and arrange the reserved pecans over.

4. Reduce the heat to 180C/350F/Gas Mark 4 and bake for a further 30 minutes or until deep golden brown and set. Serve warm with cream or ice cream.

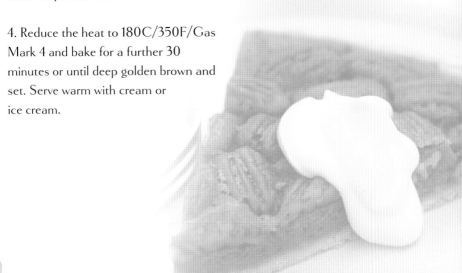

Rhubarb Crumble (Serves 6)
Ingredients
450g/1 lb rhubarb
55ml water
110g/4oz caster sugar
200g/7oz plain flour
110g/4oz cold butter, cubed
125g/4 1/4oz demerara sugar

Method

1. Preheat the oven to 180C/350F/Gas Mark 4. Trim the rhubarb into pieces about 3cm in length and place in a large ovenproof dish. Sprinkle over the water and caster sugar.

2. Sift the flour into a bowl, add the cold, cubed butter and rub in with your fingertips until the mixture resembles breadcrumbs. Stir in the demerara sugar.

3. Spread the crumble topping over the rhubarb then bake for 35-40 minutes or until the top is golden brown and the rhubarb bubbling through at the edges. Serve with cream, custard or ice cream.

Rice Pudding (Serves 4)
Ingredients
55g/1/4 cup of short grain rice
900ml/4 cups of milk
55g/1/4 cup of caster sugar
3 tbsps butter
nutmeg, for dusting (optional)

Method

1. Preheat the oven to 180C/330F/Gas Mark 4. Grease an ovenproof dish with the butter. Place the caster sugar, lemon rind and rice in the buttered dish and pour over the milk. If you are using nutmeg, shake on top.

2. Place in the oven and bake for 1 hour, stirring occasionally. Turn down the temperature to 170C/325F/Gas Mark 3 and bake for another 45 minutes. Remove from the oven and dot with a little butter.

Treacle Tart (Serves 2)

Ingredients

5 to 6 tbsps golden syrup (substitute light corn syrup)
50g/2oz fresh white breadcrumbs
finely grated rind of 1/2 to 1 lemon
1 tsp lemon juice
150g/5oz rich shortcrust pastry

Method

1. Put the syrup into a saucepan with the breadcrumbs, lemon rind and juice and heat gently until just melted. Allow to cool.

2. Roll out the dough and use to line a 20cm (8in) pie plate. Pour in the syrup mixture. Roll out the dough trimmings and cut into long narrow strips.

3. Lay these in a lattice pattern over the filling. Bake in a preheated moderately hot oven 200C/400F/Gas Mark 6 for 25 to 30 minutes or until the pastry is lightly browned.

Almond & Apricot Tart (Serves 6-8)

Ingredients for pastry

250g/2 cups plain flour
200g/1 1/2 cups melted butter
60g/1/2 cup sugar
2 egg yolks
1 pinch salt

Ingredients for filling

1 kg apricots
50g/1/2 cup sugar
50g/1/3 cup butter
75g ground almonds
1 egg
300g whole almonds
3 tbsps lavender honey

Method

1. To make the pastry, mix all ingredients together, then roll into a ball. Leave to chill for at least an hour, then roll out, then line a greased flan dish.

2. To make the filling, mix the sugar, butter, egg and ground almonds together. Spread mixture onto flan. Remove stones from apricots, cut in half and arrange on flan. Arrange whole almonds amongst apricots.

3. Bake for 55 minutes at 200C/400F/Gas Mark 6. After 30 minutes, gently heat honey. Once the tart has been taken out of the oven, drizzle the honey over the top and and place under the grill to caramelise.

4. Serve warm or cold.

Almond Tartlets with Raspberry Jam (Makes 12)

Ingredients for the tartlets

50g/1/2 cup butter
50g/1/2 cup caster sugar
50g ground almonds

Almond Tartlets with Raspberry Jam/cont.

Ingredients for the topping

50ml/1/4 cup raspberry jam

75ml/1/3 cup double cream (whipped)

Method

1. To make the tartlets; preheat the oven to 180C/350F/Gas Mark 4. Cream the butter really well until it is very soft. Add the sugar and ground almonds, and stir to combine, but do not beat. Place teaspoonfuls of this mixture into the tin, there's no need to spread it out.

2. Place in the preheated oven and cook for about 6-10 minutes until a deep golden colour. Keep an eye on them as they burn easily!

3. Let them sit in the tin for 2 minutes, before removing to a wire tray to cool. If they cool completely in the tin, they will stick. If that happens, just pop them back in the oven to 'unstick' themselves!

4. To serve, arrange the tartlets on a plate. Spread 1 tsp raspberry jam, then a little dollop of whipped cream on each, and serve.

Apple & Blackberry Pie (Serves 4)

Ingredients

300g/12oz shortcrust pastry

700g/1 1/2 lb apples

450g/1lb blackberries

sugar to taste

Method

1. Roll out the pastry and line a pie dish, reserving enough for a lid. Peel and slice the apples and carefully wash the blackberries.

2. Mix them together in the pie and add sugar and a touch of cinnamon if desired, and cover the pie.

3. Glaze and bake at 200C/400F/Gas Mark 6 for 10 - 15 minutes, then for a further 25 - 30 minutes at 180C/350F/Gas Mark 4.

Apple & Currant Pastries (Serves 4)
Ingredients for pastry
150g/1 1/2 cups plain flour

1 1/2oz lard

pinch of salt

3 tbsps margarine

Ingredients for fruit mixture
4 tsps lard

1 medium-sized cooking apple (chopped)

100g/4oz currants

1/2 tsp cinnamon

50g/1/4 cup caster sugar (superfine granulated)

Method
1. Make the pastry by rubbing 2 tbsps lard and the margarine into the flour and salt as for shortcrust pastry. Roll out the pastry and cut 12 circles using a 10cm/4in cutter.

2. Place a small spoonful of the fruit mixture in the centre of each circle. Moisten the edges of the pastry and fold over to form a half-circle shape.

3. Press the edges together with the prongs of a fork and bake for about 20 minutes at 220C/425F/Gas Mark 7 until golden brown, and serve.

Apple & Strawberry Crumble (Serves 4)
Ingredients
450g of cooking apples (cored, peeled and sliced)

225g/1 cup of strawberries (hulled & halved)

2 tbsps sugar

1/2 tsp ground cinnamon

2 tbsps orange juice

3 tbsps of plain wholemeal flour

55g/1/2 cup of porridge oats

25g low fat spread

custard or cream (to serve)

Apple & Strawberry Crumble/cont.
Method
1. Preheat the oven to 180C/350F/Gas Mark 4. Place the apples, strawberries, sugar, cinnamon and orange juice in a bowl and toss well. Tip the contents into an ovenproof dish.

2. Combine the flour and oats in a bowl and mix in the low fat spread with a fork. Sprinkle the crumble mix evenly over the fruit, (this won't cover it all completely – so for a more complete coverage increase the crumble mixture ingredients).

3. Bake in the centre of the oven for 40-45 minutes, until golden brown and bubbling. Serve warm with either custard or cream.

Blueberry & Plum Pie (Serves 8)
Ingredients for pastry
400g/14oz plain flour
200g/7oz chilled butter (diced)
3 tbsps icing sugar
1 medium egg (lightly beaten)
2 tbsps cold water

Ingredients for filling
500g plums (halved cored and cut into chunky wedges)
200g/7oz blueberries
100g/4oz caster sugar
1/2 tsp ground cinnamon
2 tbsps milk
2 tbsps granulated sugar

Method
1. Put the flour and butter into a processor and blend it until the mixture resembles breadcrumbs. Add the icing sugar, egg and cold water and blend again until the mixture forms a ball. Wrap and chill for 15 minutes.

2. Heat the oven to 200C/400F/Gas Mark 6. Gently mix together the plums, blueberries, sugar and cinnamon in a bowl.

3. Take a large sheet of baking parchment and roll out the chilled pastry on this using a floured rolling pin, to a 30cm (12in) circle. Lift the paper and pastry onto a baking sheet.

4. Pile the prepared fruit into the centre of the pastry and fold the pastry edges up and over the fruit. Brush the pastry edges with milk and sprinkle the pastry with the granulated sugar. Bake for 40 minutes until the pastry is golden and the fruit tender. Serve with single cream.

Blueberry Tart (Serves 4-6)
Ingredients for the Tart

sweet shortcrust pastry for a 22cm flan tin
50g/2oz ground almonds

Ingredients for the Filling

400g/14oz blueberries (frozen)
140g/5oz caster sugar
2 tbsps Cointreau
100g/4oz butter
3 eggs
2 tbsps cornflour or potato flour (sifted)
65 ml/2 1/2 fl oz double cream
2 tsps orange zest
2 tbsps lemon juice
50g/2oz icing sugar

Method

1. Defrost the fruit and drain off the surplus juice. Line the base and 2cm/1in up the sides of a greased flan tin with shortcrust pastry, prick all over with a fork. Chill.

2. Make the filling. Drop the blueberries, 3 tbsps sugar, liqueur and 15g (1/2oz) butter into a pan, heat and stir gently until the fruit has slightly caramelized. Leave to cool.

3. Beat together the remaining butter and caster sugar until pale and fluffy; whisk in the eggs one at a time, add the flour and cream.

Blueberry Tart/cont.

4. Mix in the orange zest and lemon juice, then fold in the blueberry mixture. Scatter the ground almonds over the base of the pastry shell and pour in the prepared filling.

5. Dredge with icing sugar and bake in the preheated oven at 180C/350F/Gas Mark 4 for 1 hour. Leave to cool in the tin.

Cheesecake Crumble

Ingredients for cheesecake

4 eggs
100g/3 1/2oz caster sugar
1 tsp vanilla essence
360g/12oz natural full fat fromage frais
300g/10oz soft cream cheese

Ingredients for crumble

12 small butter biscuits, crushed
3 tbsps rolled oats
50g/2oz butter, melted
1 tbsp brown sugar
pinch of salt

Method

1. Preheat the oven to 120C/250F/Gas Mark 1. Beat the eggs with the sugar until light and fluffy. Add the vanilla essence, fromage frais and cream cheese.

2. Pour the mixture into an ovenproof porcelain dish. Bake in the preheated oven for 45-50 minutes, until the centre is firm to the touch. Turn off the oven and leave the cheese cake in the oven until it is quite cold. Remove from the oven and refrigerate for at least 2 hours or preferably overnight.

3. Prepare the crumble topping by mixing all the ingredients lightly together. Spread the topping over the cheesecake, pressing lightly, then leave in the refrigerator until ready to serve. Serve with red fruit coulis.

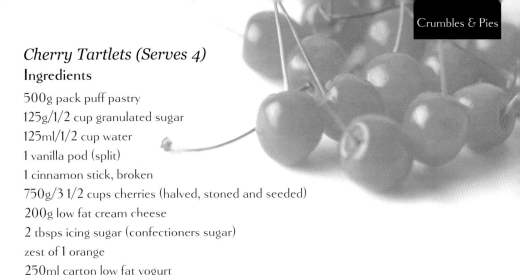

Cherry Tartlets (Serves 4)

Ingredients

500g pack puff pastry
125g/1/2 cup granulated sugar
125ml/1/2 cup water
1 vanilla pod (split)
1 cinnamon stick, broken
750g/3 1/2 cups cherries (halved, stoned and seeded)
200g low fat cream cheese
2 tbsps icing sugar (confectioners sugar)
zest of 1 orange
250ml carton low fat yogurt
4 tbsps redcurrant jelly

Method

1. Preheat the oven to 220C/450F/Gas Mark 7. On a floured surface, roll out the pastry until it is large enough to cut out six 12 x 12cm squares.

2. Upturn 6 ramekin dishes and place on a baking tray, lay the pastry on top of the ramekins and press down over the sides. Place a lightweight cooking rack over the top.

3. Bake in the oven for 10 minutes until the pastry is golden and well risen. Remove from the oven and take off the ramekin dishes, return the pastry cases to the oven for 5 minutes to dry out.

4. Dissolve the sugar and water over a low heat in a medium size saucepan with the vanilla pod and cinnamon stick. Add the cherries and poach gently over a low heat for 5 minutes. Remove the cherries with a slotted spoon and put to one side to cool.

5. Heat the remaining syrup and bring to the boil, allowing the liquid to reduce by a half. Add the redcurrant jelly and return to the boil, stirring continually until the jelly has dissolved.

6. Mix the creamery cheese with the icing sugar, orange zest and yogurt. Divide the mixture between the pastry cases, top with cherries and brush over with hot redcurrant jelly. Chill, if not being eaten immediately.

Coconut Macaroon Tart (Serves 6-8)

Ingredients

200g plain flour (sifted)
225g/2 cups butter
2 tbsps raspberry jam, (optional)
4 eggs
225g caster sugar
1 tsp ground cinnamon
150g/1 cup desiccated coconut,
icing sugar, for dusting

Method

1. For the pastry, put the flour, butter and a pinch of salt in a food processor and process briefly.

2. Add half the beaten egg and continue to process. (You might add a little more egg, but not too much as the mixture should be just moist enough to come together.) If making the pastry by hand, rub the butter into the flour until it resembles coarse breadcrumbs then, using your hands, add just enough egg to bring it together.

3. With your hands, flatten out the ball of dough until it is about 2cm thick, then wrap it in cling film or place it in a plastic bag and leave in the fridge for at least 30 minutes or, if you are pushed for time, in the freezer for 10–15 minutes, before using.

4. Preheat the oven to 180C/350F/Gas Mark 4. Line a 23cm diameter tart tin with the shortcrust pastry and cover the base with baking parchment. Fill the tin with baking beans and bake blind for 10-15 minutes. Remove the beans and parchment for the last five minutes of baking for a golden crust.

5. For the filling, whisk the eggs, sugar and cinnamon together in a bowl. Add the desiccated coconut and the melted butter and mix well. Cover the cooled base with raspberry jam before pouring in the filling and baking in the oven for 40–45 minutes, or until golden brown and just set in the centre. Remove the tart from the oven and allow to stand in the tin for about 10 minutes before carefully removing and allowing to cool on a wire rack.

Crunchy Crumble (Serves 4)
Ingredients
275g/10oz porridge oats
25g/1oz butter
60g/4 tbsps soft brown sugar
30ml/2 tbsps honey
110g/4oz raisins
50g/2oz chopped hazelnuts

Method
1. Preheat oven to 230C/450F/Gas 8. Melt the butter, sugar and honey in a saucepan, add the remaining ingredients and mix thoroughly.

2. Turn the mixture onto a greased baking tray and bake for 15 minutes or until well browned and crisp. Leave to cool, then crumble and store in an airtight container. Serve with yoghurt or ice cream.

Fig Crumble (Serves 4)
Ingredients
2 tbsps butter
2 figs, quartered
2 tbsps caster sugar
1 sprig of fresh rosemary

Ingredients for crumble topping
55g/2oz butter
30g/1oz caster sugar
30g/1oz rolled oats
30g/1oz flour
2 tbsp hazelnuts, crushed

Method
1. Preheat oven to 250C/500F/Gas 9. Melt the butter in a medium, ovenproof frying pan. Add the figs, sugar and rosemary and sauté for 3-4 minutes.

2. Melt the butter for the crumble topping in a small frying pan. Add the caster sugar and the oats and cook for 2-3 minutes. Add the flour and nuts and cook for one minute.

Fig Crumble/cont.

3. Tip the crumble topping over the figs. Place the fig crumble in the oven and bake for 4-5 minutes, or until the crumble is crisp. Serve hot, with Greek yoghurt.

Fig Tart (Serves 6)
Ingredients

sweet pastry case, or 350g pastry
1.6 kg figs
200g/2 cups sugar
150g/1 cup butter

Method

1. Roll out the pastry, cook blind for fifteen minutes, then leave to cool. Arrange figs in pastry case.

2. Cut a small cross in the top of each fig, and put in a little butter. Sprinkle with sugar. Bake for 35 minutes at 200C/400F/Gas Mark 6.

Lemon Pie (Serves 4-6)

Ingredients

110ml/1/2 cup of fresh lemon juice
9in ready-made pie crust
3 egg yolks
400ml condensed milk (sweetened)
1 tsp yellow food colouring
whipped cream (for topping)
lemon slices (for topping)

Method

1. Preheat the oven to 160C/325F/Gas Mark 3. Place the eggs, lemon juice, food colouring and condensed milk in a bowl and beat together. Transfer the mixture into the pie crust and place in the oven. Bake for 25-30 minutes.

2. Remove from the oven and allow to cool. Refrigerate for 1 hour and then garnish with the whipped cream and lemon slices.

Orange & Clementine Tart (Serves 6)

Ingredients

100g/3/4 cup butter
50g/1/2 cup sugar
1 kg clementines
2 oranges
250g sweet pastry, sweet pastry case or flaky pastry

Method

1. Put butter and sugar in a thick-bottomed pan. Peel the clementines and oranges and cut into quarters. Place in a pan. Cook for 15 minutes over a high heat.

2. If using pastry, roll out onto a floured surface, then place into flan dish. Preheat oven to 220C/450F/Gas Mark 7, and pour fruit and butter mixture into flan or pastry case. Bake for 25 minutes.

Peach & Vanilla Filo Tarts (Makes 8)

Ingredients

4 sheets filo pastry

3 tbsps butter

50g/2oz golden caster sugar

250g tub mascarpone

3 tbsps unrefined muscovado sugar

1 tsp vanilla bean paste

2 fresh peaches, sliced

3 tbsps apricot glaze

Method

1. Preheat oven to 190C/375F/Gas Mark 5. Grease a bun tin. Open out the filo pastry sheets and cut the stack into eight equal squares.

2. Lay one pastry square into a bun tin, lightly brush with butter and then scatter over a little sugar. Place a second piece of pastry over the first to form a star shape, repeat with the brushing and scattering and then top with a third and fourth piece, brushing with butter and sprinkling with sugar. Make 7 more tarts in the same way.

3. Bake for 10 minutes until they are golden brown. Allow to cool in the tins. Meanwhile mix the mascarpone cheese with the light muscovado sugar and vanilla bean paste.

4. Spoon the cheese mixture between the tartlets, arrange 4 peach slices on top of each tart.

5. Warm the apricot glaze in the microwave for 30 seconds, and then brush over the peaches to glaze. Serve within 1 hour of filling.

Plum Pie (Serves 6)

Ingredients

14 blue plums (halved and pitted)
1/2 cup brown sugar
1/2 cup white sugar
1/2 tsp of cardamon
pinch of salt
2 tbsps quick-cooking tapioca
2 tbsps lemon juice
1 tbsp butter
pastry for one crust pie.

Method

1. Fill a 9 x 9in baking dish about three-quarters full with the plums, placed cut side down. Combine the brown sugar, white sugar, cardamon, salt and tapioca and sprinkle over the plums.

2. Shake the dish slightly so that the sugar will sift down through the fruit. Sprinkle with the lemon juice and dot with the butter.

3. Bake at 190C/375F/Gas Mark 5 for 20 minutes. Roll the pastry and cut nine 3in circles from it. Remove the pie from the oven and place the circles of pastry over the fruit in a slightly overlapping design.

4. Return the pie to the oven and bake for a further 20 minutes or until the fruit is tender and the pastry brown.

Pumpkin Tart with Rum & Bitter Chocolate (Serves 4-6)

Ingredients

350-400g pumpkin (skin and seeds removed, flesh cut into small chunks)
250g/2 cups sugar
3 tbsps butter
6 tbsps rum
225g dark chocolate (roughly chopped)
75g/3/4 cup caster sugar
1 egg (lightly beaten)
150g/1 1/2 cups plain flour

Method

1. First make the pastry. Cream the butter and the sugar in a food processor until pale and fluffy. Slowly add the egg and then the flour, and pulse briefly until mixed. Roll into a ball, wrap in cling film and put in the fridge for 30 minutes.

2. Preheat the oven to 200C/400F/Gas Mark 6. Grease a 20cm flan tin.

3. Roll out the pastry thinly and press it into the tin. Trim the edges neatly. Line with baking parchment and weigh down with baking beans. Bake blind for about 5 minutes or until the pastry is a light golden brown. Remove the baking parchment and beans, and set aside.

4. Place the prepared pumpkin on a roasting tray and bake in the oven for 20-30 minutes until tender.

5. Put the sugar in a large heavy-based frying pan over low heat. Stir constantly, until the sugar turns a very dark, golden colour. Add the pumpkin and roll it around in the caramel.

6. Stir in the butter and the rum. Continue to stir until everything is well blended.

7. Spoon the mixture into the pastry case with the coarsely chopped chocolate in the middle. Bake for 10 minutes.

Quince Turnovers (Serves 8-10)

Ingredients

500g quince (peeled, cored and roughly chopped)
1/2 lemon, juice only
40g unsalted butter
pinch of salt
80g caster sugar
2 tbsps cold water
100g hazelnuts
2 sheets ready rolled puff pastry
2 egg whites (lightly beaten)
1 tbsp granulated sugar

Method

1. Preheat oven to 180C/350F/Gas Mark 4. Place the quince in a pan with the lemon juice, butter, salt, caster sugar and water.

2. Cover with a lid, bring to the boil, reduce the heat and cook gently until the quince has softened and turned to pulp. Stir from time to time to stop it burning. Remove from the heat and leave to cool.

3. Put the hazelnuts in a small baking tray and roast in a hot oven for 10 minutes, then remove and while still hot put into a tea towel and rub the skins from the nuts. Add the skinned nuts to the quince puree.

4. Cut discs out of the puff pastry using a small saucer as a guide. Spoon a dollop of the filling to one side of each disc of pastry. Brush with a little of the egg white and seal the pastry to form a semi-circle.

5. Brush the tops of the turnovers with the remaining egg white, sprinkle well with granulated sugar and pierce each turnover with the point of a knife.

6. Place a baking tray lined with parchment and cook in the hot oven for about 20 minutes until puffed and cooked through.

Raspberry Meringue Pie (Serves 6 - 8)

Ingredients for pie

150g/1 1/2 cups plain flour (plus extra to dust)
2 tbsps caster sugar
75g butter (cubed and chilled)
1 large egg yolk

Ingredients for raspberry filling

800g fresh raspberries
5 tbsps cornflour
4 tbsps butter
100g golden caster sugar, to taste
2 tbsps lemon juice
5 large egg yolks

Ingredients for meringue topping

3 large egg whites
175g golden caster sugar

Method

1. Whizz the flour, sugar and butter in a processor, until they resemble crumbs. Add the yolk and 1 tablespoon cold water, then pulse until it comes together to form a dough. Wrap in cling film and chill for 15 minutes.

2. Preheat the oven to 190C/375F/Gas Mark 5. Roll out the pastry on a floured surface and use to line a deep, 23cm fluted flan tin. Line with baking paper and fill with baking beans or rice. Place on a baking sheet and bake for 15 minutes.

3. Remove the beans and paper and bake for a further 10-12 minutes, or until dry and pale golden. Set aside to cool. Reduce the oven temperature to 180C/350F/Gas Mark 4.

4. Make the filling. Whizz the raspberries to a purée, then pass through a sieve to remove the seeds – you should end up with 675ml-700ml purée. Pour into a saucepan.

5. In a bowl, mix the cornflour with 100g sugar, the lemon juice and 1 tablespoon water to give a paste. Stir into the purée, place over a medium heat and cook, stirring, until just boiling. Cook for 1 minute, stirring continuously, until thickened.

6. Taste and add the extra sugar if the raspberries are too tart. Remove from the heat and beat in the egg yolks and butter. Cool slightly, then pour into the pastry case and chill for 30 minutes to firm up the filling.

7. Make the topping. Whisk the egg whites to soft peaks in a large, grease-free bowl. Gradually whisk in the sugar, until you have a stiff, glossy meringue. Pile on top of the filling, swirling the meringue with a palette knife to get craggy peaks. Bake for 8-10 minutes, or until the meringue is pale golden. Serve immediately.

Rhubarb Tart (Serves 8)

Ingredients
900g/2lbs rhubarb, cut into 2.5cm (1in) pieces
525g/1lb 3oz caster sugar
120g/4oz butter
3 eggs
2 tbsps white wine
250g/9oz plain flour
2 tsps baking powder
140ml/1/4 pint soured cream
1 tsp ground cinnamon
60g/2oz ground almonds
icing sugar, to dredge

Method
1. Put the rhubarb into a bowl and sprinkle with 400g (14oz) of the sugar. Cover and allow to stand for 1 - 2 hours. Cream the butter with 90g (3oz) of the remaining sugar, until it is light and fluffy.

2. Beat one of the eggs and add this and the wine to the creamed butter and sugar. Sift in the flour and baking powder and mix together well.

Rhubarb Tart/cont.

3. Knead the base mixture together until it forms a smooth dough. Wrap the dough in greaseproof paper and chill for 30 minutes in the refrigerator.

4. Roll out the dough on a lightly floured board and use it to line a well-greased, loose-based, or spring-clip, 25cm (10in) round flan tin, pressing the pastry well into the base and up the sides of the tin.

5. Strain the rhubarb and arrange the pieces in the pastry case. Bake in a preheated oven, 180C/350F/Gas Mark 4, for 30 minutes.

6. Beat together the cream and the remaining eggs and sugar. Stir in the cinnamon and ground almonds, mixing well to ensure they are thoroughly blended.

Apple & Brandy Ice Cream Shells (Serves 4)

Ingredients

170ml/3/4 cup of double cream
4 eating apples
3 tbsps brandy
25g sugar
juice and grated rind of 1/2 lemon
1 tbsp water

Method

1. Cut off the tops of the apples and hollow out the apple flesh, leaving a 1cm shell. Brush over the cut edges with lemon juice, (to prevent browning), cover and chill.

2. Chop the removed apple flesh and place in a saucepan, followed by the grated lemon rind and water. Cook for a few minutes, until tender. Transfer the apple mixture to a food processor and blend until pureed. Scoop out into a bowl and stir in the brandy and sugar. Leave to cool.

3. Whip the double cream, until slightly stiff and fold into the cooled apple and brandy mixture. Transfer to a freezer safe container and freeze for 1 1/2 hours.

4. Remove from the freezer and beat the mixture until smooth and refreeze for about 2 hours, (until half frozen). Remove from the freezer, stir and spoon into the apple shells.

6. Place the apple shells into the freezer, (open), and freeze for 6-7 hours, until firm. Remove from the freezer for 20-30 minutes to soften a little prior to serving. If not serving as soon as the apple shells are frozen, place each of the apples in individual freezer-safe bags and keep in the freezer.

Banana Splits (Serves 6)
Ingredients
450g vanilla ice cream
225ml/1 cup of double cream
6 large bananas
6 glace cherries
35-40g walnuts (chopped)

Method
1. Whip the double cream in a bowl, until slightly stiff. Peel and split the bananas lengthways and fill with equal amounts of ice cream. Sandwich the two halves together on each and place on individual serving plates.

2. Top the bananas with the whipped cream and sprinkle with chopped walnuts. Pop a cherry on top of each! Serve immediately with chocolate dessert sauce.

Buttermilk Vanilla Ice Cream (Serves 6)
Ingredients
225ml/1 cup of buttermilk
4 tbsps double cream
2 eggs
1/2 tsp vanilla essence
2 tbsps clear honey

Method
1. Place the cream and buttermilk in a saucepan and heat over a gently heat, until almost boiling. Remove from the heat.

2. Place the eggs in a bowl and place over a pan of hot water, whisk the eggs until pale and creamy. Gradually pour the warmed buttermilk/cream mixture into the bowl, whisking continuously. Whisk until slightly thickened.

3. Whisk in the vanilla essence and clear honey. Spoon into a freezer-safe container, cover and freeze until firm.

4. Remove from the freezer 20 minutes before serving, to soften. Serve with fresh fruit or fruit puree.

Chocolate Mint Ice Cream (Serves 8)

Ingredients

300ml/1 1/3 cups of milk
55g/1/4 cup of caster sugar
6 egg yolks
300g After Eight mints (or similar soft, dark chocolate mints)
560ml/2 1/2 cups of double cream

Method

1. Break the chocolate mints into small pieces and chill. Place the milk and cream in a saucepan and heat gently, until almost to boiling point. Remove from the heat.

2. Place the sugar and egg yolks in a bowl and beta together, until creamed. Gradually pour the cream/milk mixture over the eggs, whisking continuously.

3. Return the mixture to the pan and heat gently, stirring continuously, until slightly thickened. Strain the mixture through a sieve, into a bowl. Leave to cool completely. Pour into a freezer-safe container and freeze for 2-3 hours, until partly frozen. Stir the mixture and return to the freezer. Repeat this process twice more.

4. On the last occasion, stir in the chocolate mints, folding them in evenly. Return to the freezer for 7-8 hours, until firm. Remove from the freezer for 20-30 minutes to soften a little prior to serving.

Chocolate Raisin & Liqueur Ice Cream (Serves 6)

Ingredients

750ml/3 1/3 cups of double cream
300ml/1 1/3 cups of milk
4 tbsps Irish Cream Liqueur
2 eggs
75g/1/2 cup of raisins (chopped)
75g plain chocolate (broken into pieces)
55g/1/4 cup of soft brown sugar

Method

1. Place the chopped raisins in a bowl and pour the liqueur over the top. Leave to stand.

2. Place 60ml of the milk in a saucepan and add the chocolate. Warm gently, melting the chocolate. Once melted, whisk in the remaining milk. Do not boil.

3. Place the sugar and eggs in a bowl and beat together, until light and creamy. Pour in the chocolate milk, stirring in well. Return to the saucepan and cook gently, until slightly thickened.

4. Strain the liquid through a sieve over the raisin/liqueur mixture. Combine well and leave to cool completely. Whip the double cream lightly and stir into the cooled chocolate-raisin mixture.

5. Pour into a freezer-safe container and freeze for 2-3 hours. Stir the mixture, mixing the raisins throughout the ice-cream evenly and return to the freezer for 7-8 hours, until firm. Remove from the freezer for 20-30 minutes to soften a little prior to serving.

Citrus & Yoghurt Jelly (Serves 6)
Ingredients
500ml/2 cups of natural yoghurt
750ml lime jelly
zest of 1 lime
slices of lemon (to garnish)

Method
1. Make the lime jelly, as per packet instructions and refrigerate in a large bowl.

2. Just prior to setting, whisk in the natural yoghurt. Spoon into 6 dessert glasses and refrigerate. Leave to set. Once set, sprinkle with a little lime zest and garnish with lemon slices.

Coffee Ice Cream (Serves 8)
Ingredients
375ml/1 2/3 cups of double cream
375ml/1 2/3 cups of milk
150g/2/3 cup of caster sugar
1 1/2 tbsps custard powder
3 tbsps strong black coffee

Method
1, Place the custard powder in a bowl with a little bit of the milk. Place the remaining milk in saucepan and heat to almost boiling point. Pour onto the custard mixture and mix.

2. Return to the pan and simmer gently, stirring continuously, until the mixture thickens. Remove from the heat and stir in 50g of the sugar, stirring in until melted. Whip the cream in a bowl and add the hot custard mixture. Stir in the remaining sugar and black coffee. Combine well and leave to cool completely.

3. Pour into a freezer-safe container and freeze for 2-3 hours, until partly frozen. Stir the mixture and return to the freezer for 7-8 hours, until firm. Remove from the freezer for 20-30 minutes to soften a little prior to serving.

Double Chocolate-Chip Ice Cream (Serves 4)

Ingredients

150ml/2/3 cup of milk
150ml/2/3 cup of double cream
100g luxury Belgian chocolate
25g milk chocolate
30g/1/8 cup of caster sugar
2 egg yolks
1/2 tsp coffee essence

Method

1. Chop the Belgian and milk chocolate into small pieces, but keeping them separate.

2. Place 75g of the dark chocolate, 75ml of milk and the coffee essence into a bowl and heat over a saucepan of simmering water.

3. Stir the mixture until the chocolate is melted, then remove from the heat and stir in the remaining milk.

4. Mix the sugar and egg yolks together until thick in consistency and blend in the chocolate milk. Pour the mix into a saucepan and heat over a medium heat for 4-5 minutes, or until the mixture starts to thicken. Be careful not to boil. Strain the mixture into a bowl and cool until cold.

5. Once cold, add the cream into the mixture and stir well. Pour into a freezer-safe tray or bowl and freeze until half-frozen. Remove from the freezer and stir in the remaining chocolate pieces, (25g dark chocolate, 25g milk chocolate), until the mixture is thick.

6. Return to the freezer and leave for at least 3 hours. Before serving, transfer to the refrigerator for 20 minutes to soften.

Fresh Citrus Jelly (Serves 4)

Ingredients

3 oranges

1 lemon

1 lime

300ml/1 1/4 cups of water

75g/3/4 cup of golden caster sugar

1 tbsp powdered gelatine

selection of chopped fruit (to decorate – optional)

Method

1. Remove the peel and the white pith from one of the oranges and carefully remove the segments. Arrange the segments in the base of a 900ml mould or rounded dish.

2. Remove some shreds of the lemon and line rinds and put to one side. Grate the remaining lemon and lime rind, as well as the rind from one orange. Place all the grated rinds in a pan with the sugar and water.

3. Heat the rind mixture gently until the sugar dissolves. Do not boil. Remove from the heat and squeeze the juice from the remaining fruits. Stir the juices into the pan.

4. Strain the liquid into a measuring jug and discard the rind. Sprinkle the gelatine over the liquid and stir in until completely dissolved.

5. Pour a little of the mixture over the orange segments arranged in the dish and refrigerate in order to set. Leave the remaining jelly at room temperature to cool, but do not allow to set.

6. Once the refrigerated jelly has set, pour over the cooled liquid and return to the refrigerator to set completely.

7. To serve, turn out the jelly onto a plate and garnish the sides with chopped fruit of your choice, (optional). Sprinkle the reserved citrus rind over the top and sides for extra decoration.

Frozen Yoghurt with Cherry Sauce (Serves 4)

Ingredients

75ml/1/3 cup of double cream
180ml/3/4 cup of natural yoghurt
1 egg white
170g/3/4 cup of cherries (pitted)
60g/1/2 cup of caster sugar
75ml/1/3 cup of water
1 tsp arrowroot
1 tbsp icing sugar
grated dark chocolate (to serve)

Method

1. Place the water, caster sugar and cherries in a pan and bring to the boil. Reduce the heat and simmer for 4 minutes.

2. Remove from the heat, strain the juices and reserve. Remove 3-4 cherries, slice and place to one side. Place the remaining cherries in a food processor and blend until pureed. Press the cherries through a sieve into a bowl and leave to one side for 2-3 minutes.

3. Place the cream in a bowl and lightly whip. Stir into the cherry puree, followed by the yoghurt. Mix well. Place the eggs in a bowl and whisk until stiffened. Add the icing sugar and whisk again, until peaks form. Carefully fold into the cherry/yoghurt mixture. Transfer to a freezer-safe container and freeze for 3-4 hours, until firm.

4. Place the arrowroot in a bowl and add a little water to make a paste. Stir into the reserved cherry juice and add the cherry slices. Transfer to a saucepan and bring to the boil, reduce the heat and simmer for 3-4 minutes, until thickened.

5. Remove from the heat and leave to cool. Once cooled, cover and refrigerate. Remove the frozen cherry yoghurt from the freezer and place in the refrigerator for 1 1/2 -2 hours, to soften.

6. Spoon the yoghurt into serving bowls and top with the cherry sauce. Sprinkle over with dark chocolate and serve immediately.

Irish Cream & Mascarpone Ice Cream (Serves 4-6)

Ingredients

150ml/2/3 cup of double cream
280g/1 1/4 cups of mascarpone
110ml/1/2 cup of Irish Cream Liqueur
150g/2/3 cup of sugar
225ml/1 cup of water

Method

1. Heat the water in a saucepan and add the sugar, dissolve over a gentle heat. Bring to the boil and simmer for 4-5 minutes. Remove from the heat and leave to cool.

2. Place the mascarpone in a bowl and stir in the liqueur, mix together until smooth. Stir in the double cream and gradually add the cooled sugar syrup, stirring continuously.

3. Pour the mixture into a freezer-proof container and place in the freezer for 1-2 hours. Stir the mixture and return to the freezer for another 1-2 hours. Stir again and then return to the freezer for 7-8 hours, until firm.

4. Remove from the freezer for 20-30 minutes to soften a little prior to serving.

Mango Sorbet (Serves 4)

Ingredients

250g/1 cup of plain yoghurt
2 small mangoes (peeled and cubed)
2 tsps sugar

Method

1. Place the mango and sugar into a food processor and blend until smooth. Add in the yoghurt and mix.

2. Pour the mixture into a freezer-safe container and place in the freezer for at least 4 hours, whisking at regular intervals. Once frozen, spoon into dishes and serve immediately.

Knickerbocker Glory! (Makes 6)
Ingredients
250ml/1 cups of double cream
375g vanilla ice cream
375g chocolate ice cream
75g chocolate (broken into pieces)
340g/1 1/2 cups of strawberries (hulled & halved)
6 peaches (peeled & cut into thin slices)
4-6 large cherries (pitted)
5 tbsps brandy (optional)
43g/1/4 cup of chocolate chips (optional)

Method
1. Divide the strawberries equally and place at the base of 6 tall sundae glasses.

2. Place a scoop of vanilla ice cream in each glass and top with equal amounts of peach slices. Top with a scoop of chocolate ice cream.

3. Place the chocolate and brandy in a bowl and gently heat, stirring continuously. Melt and combine the chocolate with the brandy and then pour a little over the top of the chocolate ice cream.

4. Place the double cream in a bowl and beat until stiff peaks form. Spoon on top of the sundaes and decorate with cherries. Add a few chocolate chips, if you're feeling a bit naughty!

Orange Sorbet (Serves 4)

Ingredients

6 oranges

2 lemons

2 small sticks cinnamon

250g granulated sugar

300ml water

3 tbsps Cointreau

This recipe is for use with an ice cream machine.

Method

1. Place the sugar and water in a saucepan. Snap the cinnamon sticks into 2.5cm lengths and add to the sugar and water. Set over a moderate heat and stir until the sugar has dissolved, then bring up to the boil and cook for 10 minutes.

2. Meanwhile, squeeze the juice from the oranges and lemons. Put some ice and a little cold water in a large bowl. Set a slightly smaller bowl on top of the ice. As soon as the cinnamon syrup has boiled for 10 minutes, pour into the bowl and stir in the Cointreau.

3. Keep stirring, as the syrup will become increasingly thick as it cools. As soon as it is tepid, stir in the citrus juice. Once cold, strain the liquid and pour into an ice cream machine.

4. Churn the mixture according to the manufacturer's instructions until it reaches a medium set. Alternatively, pour into a shallow plastic container, cover and freeze. Beat with a fork every 40 minutes or so, until you have a smooth, even-textured sorbet with tiny ice crystals.

Summer Fruits Ice Cream (Serves 6-8)

Ingredients

900g/2 cups of soft summer fruit
(raspberries, strawberries, blackcurrants, redcurrants, blueberries)
225g/1 cup of Greek yoghurt
2 eggs
175ml/3/4 cup of red grape juice
1 tbsp powdered gelatine

Method

1. Puree half of the fruit in a food processor and rub it through a sieve into a bowl to make it a completely smooth puree. Separate the eggs and whisk the yolks and the yoghurt into the fruit puree.

2. Heat the grape juice in a pan until its almost boiling, (but do not boil). Remove from the heat and sprinkle in the gelatine; mix in until dissolved.

3. Whisk the grape juice mixture into the fruit puree mixture and pour into a freezer-safe container. Place in the freezer and freeze until half frozen and a slushy consistency.

4. Whisk the egg whites until they are stiff and quickly fold them into the half frozen mixture. Return to the freezer and freeze until almost firm.

5. To serve, scoop into dishes and add the other half of the summer fruits to taste and decorate.

Apple & Blackberry Fruit Dessert (Serves 8)

Ingredients

500g/5 cups of blackberries (frozen)
4 apples (peeled & thinly sliced)
30g butter
100g/1/2 cup of dark brown sugar
2 tsps lemon rind (grated)
125g/2 1/2 cups of soft breadcrumbs
40g/1/2 cup of toasted slivered almonds
8 tbsps whipped cream

Method

1. Spray the slow cooker with non-stick cooking spray, or grease lightly with butter.

2. Thaw the blackberries and drain; reserving the juice. Place the blackberries and apple slices in a bowl and mix together.

3. Place the brown sugar, breadcrumbs and lemon rind in a bowl and mix together. Melt the butter in a pan and add to the breadcrumb mixture, combine well.

4. Place 1/4 of the breadcrumb mixture in the base of the slow cooker and top with 1/3 of the fruit mixture. Continue this layering sequence, finishing with a layer of breadcrumbs.

5. Cover and cook on a low temperature for 5 to 6 hours. Serve in individual bowls, with whipped cream and a sprinkling of almonds.

Apple & Mixed Berry Compote

Ingredients

425g of mixed berries (raspberries, strawberries, blueberries)
3-4 apples (peeled, cored & chopped)
110ml/1/2 cup of apple juice
1/8 tsp cinnamon

Method

1. Place the apple juice, apples and cinnamon in a saucepan and cook gently for 8-10 minutes, until just softened. Add the berries and serve with pancakes, natural yoghurt or other dessert.

Apricots with Honey Yoghurt (Serves 6)

Ingredients

330ml/1 1/3 cups of natural yoghurt
120ml clear honey
30ml/1/8 cup of white wine
9 apricots (stoned & halved)
1 tbsp caster sugar

Method

1. Preheat the oven to 180C/350F/Gas Mark 4. Arrange the apricots, cut-side up, on a baking tray. Cover evenly with white wine and sprinkle over with sugar.

2. Place in the oven and bake for 15-20 minutes, until soft. Whilst the apricots are baking, place the honey in a saucepan and gently heat. Remove and place to one side.

3. Remove the apricots from the oven and divide between 6 serving bowls. Spoon over the top with warm honey and serve with yoghurt, as desired.

Banana & Berry Delight with Nutmeg (Serves 4)
Ingredients

1 tsp nutmeg
2 large bananas (or 3 small)
175g/1 1/2 cups of frozen or fresh cranberries
60g/1/2 cup of oats

Ingredients for serving

4 scoops of low-fat frozen yoghurt (optional)

Method

1. Cut the bananas into 1/2in pieces. Mix all the ingredients together in a non-stick frying pan and cook on a medium heat, stirring occasionally. Once the cranberries begin to soften, remove from the heat and leave to cool for one minute.

2. Serve the mixture into bowls and finish off with a scoop of low-fat frozen yoghurt, if desired.

Berry Ripple (Serves 8)
Ingredients

930g/3 3/4 cups of vanilla yoghurt
375g frozen mixed berry fruits (defrosted)
1 1/4 tbsps pistachios (chopped)

Method

1. Place the berry fruits in a food processor and blend until smooth.

2. Place the vanilla yoghurt in a large bowl and fold in the blended fruits, until creating a marbled-effect.

3. Divide equally between 8 dessert bowls and chill for 20 minutes. To serve, top with the chopped pistachios.

Cherry & Almond Spice Slices (Makes 24)
Ingredients
1/2 tsp ground nutmeg

2 tsps ground cinnamon

375g/1 2/3 cups of butter (softened)

395g/1 3/4 cups of glace cherries (washed, dried & chopped)

315g/2 3/4 cups of plain flour

200g/1 3/4 cups of self raising flour

340g/1 1/2 cups of caster sugar

100g ground rice

4 eggs (beaten)

2 tbsps demerara sugar

2 tbsps slivered almond flakes

Method
1. Preheat the oven to 180C/350F/Gas Mark 4. Line two 28 x 18cm baking tins with baking paper. Place the 200g of butter and 100g of caster sugar in a bowl and beat together well, until fluffy.

2. Sift the plain flour into a bowl and add the cinnamon and ground rice; gently fold together, making a soft dough. Divide equally and press into the bases of the baking tins.

3. Sprinkle the chopped cherries evenly over the surface of the dough. Place the remaining caster sugar and butter together and then fold in the self raising flour and eggs. Combine well. Spoon the mixture equally over the dough/cherries and level off the surface with the back of a spoon.

4. Sprinkle over with the almonds and demerara sugar, followed by the nutmeg. Make sure that you do this as evenly as possible.

5. Place in the oven for 35-40 minutes, until lightly browned and firm to touch. Remove from the oven and leave to cool on a wire cooling rack. Once cooled, peel the baking paper away and cut into 12 slices, per baking tray.

Citrus Meringues (Serves 4)
Ingredients for meringues
300ml/1 1/3 cups of low-fat natural yoghurt
8 ready-made meringue nests (crushed)
1/2 tsp grated lime rind
1/2 tsp grated lemon rind
2 tbsps unsweetened orange juice

Ingredients for sauce
55g/1/4 cup of kumquats (thinly sliced)
2 tbsps lemon juice
2 tbsps lime juice
2 tbsps water
2 tsps caster sugar
1 tsp cornflour (mixed with 1 tbsp water)
8 tbsps unsweetened orange juice

Method for meringues
1. Place the crushed meringues in a large bowl. Add the citrus rinds, orange juice and yoghurt and stir in well.

2. Spoon the mixture into 4 mini-serving bowls, flattening the tops. Place in the freezer for 2 hours, until firm.

Method for sauce
1. Place the sliced kumquats in a saucepan with the fruit juices and water. Place over a medium/high heat and bring to the boil. Reduce the heat and simmer gently for 4-5 minutes, until the fruit has softened.

2. Add the sugar and stir in the cornflour, stirring continuously whilst cooking. When the mixture has thickened remove from the heat and pour into a small bowl; cover with cling film and leave to cool.

3. When ready to serve the meringues, dip the meringue-filled bowls in hot water for 6-8 seconds, (until they loosen a little), and turn out onto a serving plate. Spoon a little of the sauce over the meringue and decorate the top with a slice of kumquat. Serve immediately.

Cranberry & Chocolate Pudding (Serves 2)

Ingredients

15g/1/8 cup of cranberries
1/2 apple (peeled & diced)
150g/3/4 cup of dark brown sugar
1 egg (lightly beaten)
1/4 cup of butter (softened)
30g/1/4 cup of self-raising flour
1 1/2 tbsps cocoa powder (unsweetened)
1/2 tbsp vegetable oil

Method

1. Grease 2 pudding bowls, (heat resistant), with the vegetable oil and line with baking paper. Pour an inch of hot water into the slow cook and preheat to a high temperature.

2. Place the cranberries and diced apple in a bowl and mix together. Add 1/2 tablespoon of sugar and stir in. Spoon the mixture equally into the pudding bowls and gently press down a little.

3. Place the eggs, cocoa powder, butter and remaining sugar in a bowl and beat together until smooth. Spoon the mixture over the fruit in the pudding bowls and cover over with foil.

4. Place the bowls in the slow cooker and pour in enough water to cover the sides of the bowls about 2/3 up. Cover and cook for 1 3/4 to 2 hours, until risen and firm.

5. Remove from the slow cooker and leave to cool for 20 minutes. Turn out onto a serving plate and serve with cream or hot chocolate sauce.

Mixed Fruit Compote (Serves 4)

Ingredients

450g/2 cups of dried fruits (apricots, apples, prunes, pears etc)
225g/1 cup of chopped fresh rhubarb
55g/1/2 cup of unrefined light brown sugar
110g/1/2 cup of low fat yoghurt

Method

1. Preheat the oven to 180C/350F/Gas Mark 4. Place the rhubarb in a saucepan with the sugar and 300ml, (1 1/4 cups), of water. Bring to the boil and simmer for 5 minutes.

2. Place the dried fruits in an ovenproof dish and add the rhubarb, (with its cooking liquid). Stir well.

3. Cover the dish and bake in the centre of the oven for 25 minutes, (or until the fruit has softened). Serve warm with a scoop of low-fat yoghurt.

Orange Yoghurt Brûlée (Serves 4)

Ingredients

160g/2/3 cup of Greek yoghurt
55g/1/4 cup of crème fraiche
2 medium sized oranges (peeled, segmented; membrane removed)
55g/1/4 cup of golden caster sugar
30g/1/8 cup of light muscovado sugar

Method

1. Layer the orange segments equally in four ovenproof dishes. Place the yoghurt and crème fraiche in a bowl and mix together. Spoon over the orange segments.

2. Place the caster sugar and muscovado sugar in a bowl and mix together. Sprinkle evenly over the top of the dishes.

3. Preheat the grill to a high heat. Place the dishes under the grill for 3-4 minutes, until the sugar melts and turns golden brown. Remove and serve either warm, or cold.

Pear & Pomegranate Salad (Serves 2-3)

Ingredients

1 pomegranate (skin and light-coloured membrane removed)
3 pears (peeled and cut into wedges)
1 tbsp of fresh lemon juice
2 tbsps light brown sugar
1/4 tsp ground nutmeg
1/2 tsp ground cinnamon
2 tbsps finely chopped almonds
4 sprigs fresh mint leaves

Method

1. Place the pomegranate seeds and pear slices into a bowl with the lemon juice and toss well.

2. Mix the nutmeg, brown sugar and cinnamon in a bowl and add to the fruit. Mix well.

3. Cover the mixture and refrigerate for at least one hour before serving. Serve into bowls and top with a sprinkling of chopped almonds and a sprig of mint.

Quinoa Fruit Salad (Serves 2)

Ingredients

115g/1 cup of quinoa (rinsed and drained)
225ml/1 cup of water
2 red apples, diced
1/2 tsp cinnamon
225g/1 cup of chopped celery
112g/1/2 cup of dried cranberries
112g/1/2 cup of chopped walnuts
220g/1 cup of low-fat vanilla yoghurt

Method

1. Place the quinoa, apple juice, water and cinnamon in a pan and bring to the boil. Reduce the heat and simmer until all of the liquid is absorbed, (about 10-15 minutes).

2. Remove from the heat and allow to cool, then transfer to a large mixing bowl. Cover the bowl and refrigerate for at least 1 hour.

3. Remove from the refrigerator and mix in the apples, celery, dried cranberries and walnuts. Carefully fold in the yoghurt and serve immediately.

Raspberry & Plum Delight (Serves 4)

Ingredients

225g/1 cup of raspberries (fresh or frozen)
8 fresh plums (halved)
3 cinnamon sticks (2-3in)
335ml/1 1/2 cups of red wine
110ml/1/2 cup of water
2 tbsps sugar
1 tbsp corn starch
4 scoops of low-fat frozen yoghurt
sprigs of mint (to garnish)

Method

1. Place the raspberries, plums and cinnamon in a saucepan and stir well. Bring the mixture to a boil and simmer gently for 12-15 minutes.

2. Whisk the cornstarch with the water and add to the pan. Stirring continuously, cook until mixture has thickened. Stir in the sugar, leave to cool.

3. Take out the cinnamon sticks and add the mixture to a food processor. Blend until the mixture has pureed. Pour into a bowl and refrigerate for at least 1 hour.

4. To serve, spoon equally into serving bowls and add a scoop of low-fat frozen yoghurt. Garnish with mint and serve immediately.

Raspberry Fool (Serves 4)

Ingredients

150ml/2/3 cup of double cream
170ml/2/3 cup of natural yoghurt
250g/2 cups of raspberries
60g/1/2 cup of caster sugar
4 fresh mint leaves

Method

1. Place the raspberries in a glass bowl and crush them with a fork. Add the sugar and mix together well. Leave to one side for 15 minutes.

2. Place the cream in a bowl and beat until thickened. Gradually add the yoghurt, bit by bit, beating it thoroughly.

3. Swirl the raspberry mixture into the yoghurt/cream mixture. Do not combine completely, as this will mix the colours too much.

4. Spoon into glass dessert bowls and garnish with mint. Place in the refrigerator for 2-3 hours before serving.

Savoury Apricot Halves (Serves 6)

Ingredients

6 fresh apricots (halved)
110g low-fat cream cheese (softened)
55g/1/4 cup of pistachio nuts (finely chopped)

Method

1. Stir the cream cheese until smooth. Spoon into the apricot halves and sprinkle with the chopped nuts. Serve immediately!

Spiced Fruit (Serves 4-6)

Ingredients

1 tsp ground nutmeg
1 tsp ground cinnamon
350g/1 3/4 cups of canned pineapple chunks (undrained)
700g/4 cups of canned pear slices (drained)

700g/4 cups of canned peach slices (drained)
110g/1/2 cup of maraschino cherries (drained)
425g canned mixed fruit salad
50g/1/4 cup of brown sugar
1 tbsp cornstarch
2 tbsps butter

Method

1. This recipe should be cooked in a slow cooker, but if you do not have one, cook in a conventional oven on the lowest heat possible.

2. Place all of the ingredients in the slow cooker or casserole dish and mix together well. Cover and cook for 4 to 6 hours. Serve in individual serving bowls with double cream.

Sussex Pond Pudding (Serves 4)
Ingredients

1 large lemon
350g suet crust pastry
170g demerara sugar
110g/1 cup of unsalted butter (well chilled)
15g butter (softened)

Method

1. Grease a 900ml pudding basin with butter. Roll out the suet crust pastry to a thickness of about 2.5cm and then keep back about a quarter of the pastry for the lid.

2. Line the basin with the pastry. Cut the chilled butter into 8 pieces, then place 4 of these with half of the sugar in the basin.

3. Prick the lemon with a sharp knife or skewer and then press one end into the butter and sugar mixture, so that it's standing upright.

4. Press the remaining half of the butter cubes and sugar around the top of the lemon, and then place the pastry lid on top. Trim off any excess from the lid, then dampen the edges and pinch all around the pudding basin to seal.

5. Cover with pleated greaseproof paper and foil, then place in a saucepan of boiling water and steam for 3 hours, topping up the water as necessary.

6. Carefully remove from the heat, take off the foil and greaseproof paper and place a plate on top of the pudding. Turn the pudding over, holding the plate in place to invert the pudding. Cut into wedges at the table, so that the 'pond' sauce runs out.

Tropical Fruit Salad (Serves 6-8)

Ingredients

10 cardamom pods
1 vanilla pod
2 cinnamon sticks
1 tsp arrowroot (mixed with 2 tsps water)
300ml/1 1/3 cups of orange juice
100g/1 cup of blueberries
3 kiwis (cubed)
1 mango (cubed)
415g/2 3/4 cups of melon (cubed)
2 passion fruits (flesh only)
2 tsps sugar
3-4 tbsps Grand Marnier

Method

1. Place the Grand Marnier, orange juice, sugar, vanilla pod, cardamom pods and cinnamon sticks in a saucepan and bring to the boil. Reduce the heat and simmer on a low heat for 4-5 minutes.

2. Add the blended arrowroot to the saucepan and return to the boil, stir continuously until the mixture thickens. Leave to cool.

3. Remove the whole spices and stir in the fruit. Refrigerate for 1-2 hours before serving. Serve with crème fraiche or frozen yoghurt.

Allspice & Chocolate Slices (Serves 10-12)

Ingredients

2 tsps ground allspice
16 digestive biscuits (crushed)
55g/1/4 cup of glace cherries (chopped)
50g/2/3 cup of slivered flaked almonds
100g/3/4 cup of dark chocolate (melted)
55g/1/4 cup of butter (melted)
1 tbsp orange juice

Method

1. Place the biscuits, almonds, allspice and cherries in a bowl and mix together well. Add the orange juice, melted butter and chocolate.

2. Transfer the mixture to shallow cake tin and spread evenly, smoothing the surface with the back of a spoon. Refrigerate for 2-3 hours, (or longer if preferred), until set. Cut into slices and serve.

Chocolate & Banana Mighty Mousse (Serves 8)

Ingredients

1 banana, (chopped)
200g/7oz dark chocolate
1/2 tbsp of double cream
170g/6oz mascarpone cheese
squeeze of lemon juice
1 tbsp of shredded fresh mint leaves
dash of rum (optional)

Method

1. Add the cream and chocolate into a bowl and heat over a pan of simmering water until melted.

2. Add the mascarpone, mint leaves, lemon juice, banana and rum together in a bowl; beat thoroughly until well combined. Stir in the melted chocolate.

3. Pour the mixture equally into dessert bowls and refrigerate for 30 minutes. Remove from the refrigerator and serve.

Chocolate & Coffee Dessert Pots (Serves 4)
Ingredients
300ml/1 1/3 cups of milk
150ml/2/3 cup of double cream
4 egg yolks
120g plain chocolate (broken into pieces)
1 tbsp light brown sugar
1 tsp instant coffee powder
1 tbsp coffee liqueur
Whipped cream (to serve)

Method
1. Place the sugar and instant coffee in a pan and mix together. Stir in the milk and cream and place over a medium heat to dissolve the sugar and coffee. Bring to the boil, stirring continuously.

2. Remove from the heat and stir in the chocolate and coffee liqueur. Place the egg yolks in a bowl and whisk. Gradually whisk in the chocolate/cream mixture, mixing together well.

3. Strain the mixture through a sieve into a large mixing jug and then pour into 4 individual serving pots, or ramekins. Cover each with foil.

4. Place in the slow cooker and pour in enough water to come halfway up the sides of the pots/ramekins. Cover and cook on a high temperature for 2 3/4 to 3 hours, until the dessert is set.

5. Remove from the slow cooker and remove the foil, leave to cool. Once cooled, cover and place in the refrigerator for at least 1 hour. Serve with whipped cream.

Chocolate & Orange Tartlets (Serves 8)
Ingredients for pastry
350g/12oz plain flour
170g/6oz butter (cubed)
50g/2oz caster sugar
2 egg yolks
1 tbsp of water

Ingredients for filling

2 medium sized eggs

2 egg yolks

100g/4oz caster sugar

200g/7oz dark chocolate

50g/2oz butter

2 tbsps of double cream

100ml/4fl oz orange liqueur

Method for pastry

1. Add the flour, sugar, butter and egg yolk into a food processor and blend until the mixture looks like breadcrumbs.

2. Add the water, preferably whilst the processor is going, and blend until the mixture turns into a ball of dough. Remove from the processor, wrap in cling film and leave for at least 30 minutes. Break the dough into 8 similar-sized balls and roll it out onto a floured surface to about a 2-3mm thickness. Line 8 greased tartlet cases with the pastry mix, cover over and refrigerate for 20-30 minutes.

3. Whilst the pastry is in the refrigerator pre-heat the oven to 180C/350F/Gas Mark 4. Once chilled, line each pastry case with greaseproof paper and weigh down with baking beans. Bake for 10 minutes and then remove to take off the beans and greaseproof paper. Return to the oven for 10 minutes, then leave to cool.

Method for filling

1. Whisk the egg yolk, egg and sugar together until the mixture is pale and has doubled in volume.

2. Add the butter, cream, chocolate and liqueur to a bowl and heat over a pan of hot water – be careful not to boil the water as this will separate the mixture in the bowl. Fold the melted mixture into the eggs and mix thoroughly, folding as you go.

3. Pour the mixture into the pastry cases and bake in the oven for 15 minutes. Remove from the oven and leave to cool. Once cooled remove the tartlets from their cases and serve.

Chocolate-Dream Dessert (Serves 6)

Ingredients

350g cooking chocolate (broken into pieces)
170ml/3/4 cup of double cream
4 eggs
115g/3/4 cup of toasted ground almonds
icing sugar (to dust)

Method

1. Line the base of the slow cooker with a piece of baking paper. Place the broken chocolate into a bowl and place over a saucepan of hot water. Heat until the chocolate is melted.

2. Place the eggs into a bowl and place over a saucepan of hot water for 4-5 minutes, then beat the eggs until thick.

3. Whip the cream in a separate bowl until it thickens and soft peaks form. Fold the chocolate into the eggs, followed by the cream and almonds.

4. Pour the chocolate mixture into the slow cooker, cover and cook on a low temperature for 3 1/2 to 4 hours, until the cake is set. Allow to cool for 30 minutes. Dust with icing sugar and serve with cream or a scoop of ice-cream.

Chocolate Fondue & Fruit (Serves 4-6)

Ingredients

selection of fruits (sliced)
260g/1 1/2 cups of dark chocolate (broken)
280ml/1 1/4 cups of double cream

Method

1. Put the broken chocolate into a bowl, add the cream and place in a saucepan of hot water. Place over a medium/high heat until the contents have melted. Stir together well.

2. Pour the mixture into a serving bowl and place on a large plate. Arrange the sliced fruit around the edge of the plate and provide skewers for dipping. Serve and enjoy!

Chocolate Fudge Liqueur Sauce

Ingredients

200g/7oz dark chocolate
400g/14oz condensed milk
1 tbsp golden syrup
2 tbsps Grand Marnier®
2 tbsps cold water

Directions

1. Break the chocolate into a pan and add the golden syrup, condensed milk, Grand Marnier and water. Heat and gently stir occasionally until the ingredients are melted and well mixed.

2. Pour into a jug to serve warm, or store in a container and refrigerate. To serve once refrigerated warm over a gentle heat. Use within 2 weeks of making.

Chocolate Ice Cream Cake (Serves 10-12)

Ingredients

1 1/2 litres chocolate fudge brownie ice-cream (softened)
500ml strawberry cheesecake ice-cream (softened)
200g milk chocolate

Method

1. To prepare, line the base of a 23cm spring-form tin with baking paper. Line a 2nd baking tray with baking paper.

2. Remove the ice-cream from the freezer for 20 minutes before starting. Do not re-freeze any remaining ice-cream. Spoon 1 litre of the chocolate fudge brownie ice-cream into the lined tin and spread evenly.

3. Spread the strawberry ice-cream evenly on top, then add the remaining 500ml of the chocolate fudge brownie ice-cream. Cover and place in freezer overnight.

4. Take the chocolate bar and holding over the lined baking tray, grate using either a potato peeler or side of cheese grater; making curly chocolate shavings. Refrigerate over night.

Chocolate Ice Cream Cake/cont.

5. About 20 minutes before serving, remove the ice-cream cake from the freezer. Run a knife that has been dipped into hot water around the tin. Using a palette knife, ease under the base and slide out onto a serving dish.

6. Lift the chocolate curls with a spoon and sprinkle onto the cake. Serve immediately.

Chocolate Mousse (Makes 12)

Ingredients

225g dark chocolate (broken into pieces)
310ml/1 1/4 cups of double cream
3 eggs (separated)
3 tbsps caster sugar
24 chocolate dessert decorations

Method

1. Firstly, melt the chocolate in a glass bowl either in the microwave, (on defrost setting) or over a saucepan of boiling water. Leave to cool on one side for 3-5 minutes.

2. Place the cream in a bowl and beat with an electric hand mixer, until soft peaks form.

3. Place the egg whites in a separate bowl, until soft peaks form. Add the sugar and beat for 2 minutes, until the sugar has dissolved and the mixture has thickened.

4. Stir the egg yolks into the saucepan of cooled chocolate with a metal spoon – stir until well combined. Stir 1/3 of the egg/sugar mixture into the chocolate mixture, mixing together well. Repeat twice more until combined.

5. Carefully fold in the whipped cream. Transfer the mixture into a large icing bag. Equally pipe the mixture into the dessert glasses and cover with cling wrap.

6. Chill in the refrigerator for 4-5 hours, until set. Decorate with chocolate dessert shapes and serve.

Chocolate Pudding Melt (Serves 6)

Ingredients

200g/7oz dark chocolate
60g/2 1/2oz plain flour
200g/7oz butter, (cubed)
110g/4oz golden caster sugar
4 large eggs and 4 large egg yolks
2 tbsps of brandy
2 tsps vanilla extract
single or whipped cream for pouring, or vanilla icecream

Method

1. Preheat the oven to 200C/400F/Gas Mark 6. Break the chocolate into a bowl and add the brandy and butter. Heat over a pan of just simmering water to melt slowly. Ensure that the bowl is clear of the water to ensure that the mixture does not overheat. Once melted, remove from the heat and stir until smooth.

2. Place the eggs, yolks, vanilla extract and sugar in a large bowl and whisk using a hand-held electric whisk. Whisk the mixture until it has thickened to a mousse-like texture and doubled in volume.

3. Pour in the melted chocolate down the sides of the bowl; this will make it easier to fold into the mixture. Sift the flour into the bowl and then slowly and carefully fold all the ingredients together. It will take a few minutes to be mixed thoroughly.

4. Spoon the mixture into 6 heat resistant pudding bowls and place them on a baking tray. If not needed until the next day the puddings can be covered and refrigerated.

5. Bake in the centre of oven for 12-15 minutes, or until they have risen and are firm to the touch, (the centre of the puddings will be melting). Leave to stand for 2 minutes and then turn each pudding out onto individual plates. Either serve straight away as a warm dessert with melting insides, or as a cold dessert with a fudge-like chocolate centre. Both can be served with pouring or whipped cream, or icecream.

Chocolate Slices (Serves 10-12)
Ingredients
16 digestive biscuits (crushed)
55g/1/4 cup of glace cherries (chopped)
50g/2/3 cup of slivered flaked almonds
100g/3/4 cup of dark chocolate (melted)
55g/1/4 cup of butter (melted)
1 tbsp orange juice
2 tsps ground allspice

Method
1. Place the biscuits, almonds, allspice and cherries in a bowl and mix together well. Add the orange juice, melted butter and chocolate.

2. Transfer the mixture to shallow cake tin and spread evenly, smoothing the surface with the back of a spoon. Refrigerate for 2-3 hours, (or longer if preferred), until set.

3. Cut into slices and serve.

Fruity Chocolate Cold Cake (Serves 8-12)
Ingredients
225g/2 1/4 cups of ginger nut biscuits, broken
175g dark chocolate, chopped into small pieces
25g sultanas
25g glace cherries, chopped
25g dried cherries
25g mixed peel
25g flaked almonds
150g/2/3 cup of unsalted butter
4 tbsps double cream

Method
1. Line a cake tin with foil and brush the foil lightly with oil. Place the ginger nut biscuits, fruit, peel and almonds in a bowl and combine well.

2. Place the butter, cream and chocolate in a pan and place over a low heat, stir until the chocolate is melted and the mixture is smooth.

3. Pour the melted chocolate mix over the biscuit/fruit mix in the bowl and stir together.

4. Spoon the mixture into the cake tin and press down firmly and evenly. Cover the cake mix with foil and refrigerate for 2 1/2 -3 hours.

5. Remove from the refrigerator and turn out onto a plate, peeling off the foil. To serve, cut into slices. Serve with vanilla or chocolate ice cream!

Cinnamon & Chilli Chocolate Fondue (Serves 10-12)
Ingredients
2 tsps ground cinnamon
1 tsp crushed chillies
450g milk or plain chocolate
400ml/1 3/4 cups of double cream
grated zest of 1 orange
selection of fruits for dipping

Method
1. Place the chocolate, orange zest, crushed chillies and cinnamon in a bowl and set over a pan of simmering water. Once the chocolate has melted gradually stir in the cream. Combine well.

2. Pour the mixture into a fondue or serving bowl and serve with a selection of fruits around the outside.

Mini Chocolate Souffles (Makes 12)

Ingredients for sauce

200g/7oz sugar
100g/4oz cocoa powder
200ml/7fl oz crème fraiche
12 slices candied orange

Ingredients for souffles

200g/7 oz dark chocolate
200g/7 oz icing sugar
120g/4 1/2 oz butter
65g/2 1/2 oz cocoa powder
8 eggs, separated

Method for sauce

1. Lightly grease 12 ramekins. Place the sugar and broken chocolate in a pan and heat gently. Gradually add in the crème fraiche, stirring continuously.

2. Cook until the volume is reduced by half.

Method for souffles

1. Preheat the oven to 190C/375F/Gas Mark 5. Break the chocolate into a bowl and heat over a pan of simmering water until melted. Add in the butter and egg yolks and mix.

2. Whisk the egg whites until stiff, then add in the sugar and carry on whisking. Add this to the chocolate mixture, little by little.

3. Lightly grease 12 ramekins. Spoon out the mixture into the ramekins to three-quarters full. Bake in the oven for 8-10 minutes. Do not open the door whilst cooking!

4. Remove from the oven and decorate the top with the strips of the candied orange and dust with icing sugar.

White Chocolate Meringues (Makes 16)
Ingredients
500g/16oz caster sugar
8 large egg whites
120g/4oz grated white chocolate
2-3 drops vanilla essence
1 tsp cornflour
1 tsp white wine or cider vinegar

Method
1. To prepare, line two greased baking trays with lightly oiled greaseproof paper. Preheat the oven to 100C/200F/Gas Mark 1.

2. Whip the egg whites with 1/2 the sugar until it creates stiff peaks. Gently whisk in the remaining ingredients.

3. Spoon 16 circles of the mix onto the baking trays, approximately 6-8cm in diameter. Bake in the oven for 1 to 1 1/4 hours. Remove from the oven and leave to cool. Serve with whipped cream and a variety of sliced fruits, if desired.

White Chocolate Mint Mousse (Makes 8-10)
Ingredients
300g/10oz white chocolate
65ml/2 1/2oz Crème de menthe®
6 eggs, separated
12 tsps caster sugar
12–14 mint leaves, stalks removed and finely chopped

Method
1. Break the chocolate into a bowl and heat over a pan of simmering water until melted. Add the egg whites with half of the sugar and whisk until the mixture is almost stiff. Add the remaining sugar and whisk again, until stiff.

2. Whisk in the egg yolks with the melted chocolate, followed by the Crème de menthe and fresh mint. Leave to cool for 5 minutes.

White Chocolate Mint Mousse/cont.

3. Whisk one-third of the egg white/sugar mixture into the chocolate mixture, mix well. Gently fold in the remaining amount of egg white/sugar mixture with a metal spoon, taking care not to lose too much air in the process. Spoon the mixture into tall dessert glasses or dessert bowls. Refrigerate for 30 minutes to chill. Serve with a sprig of mint on the top for decoration.

Chantilly Meringues (Makes 12)

Ingredients for meringues

260g caster sugar (unrefined)
6 egg whites (beaten)

Ingredients for filling

600ml double cream
50g caster sugar (unrefined)
3-4 drops of vanilla extract

Method for meringues

1. Preheat the oven to 140C/275F/Gas Mark 1. Line 2 baking trays with baking paper. Beat half of the sugar into the beaten eggs; followed by the remaining half – beat well.

2. Spoon the mixture onto the baking trays; 12 spoonfuls per tray. Place in the oven for 2 hours. To ensure that your meringues are crispy, turn the oven off and leave the meringues inside overnight.

Method for filling

1. Place the cream, sugar and vanilla extract in a bowl and whisk together, until soft peaks form. Place a dollop of cream onto 12 of the meringues and then top with the other 12, creating a sandwich.

2. Place in the refrigerator for 1 hour before serving.

Chocolate Cream Dream (Serves 4-6)

Ingredients

300ml/1/2 pint single cream
300ml/1/2 pint double cream
100g/4oz white breadcrumbs
115g/4 1/2oz demerara sugar
2 tbsps coffee
8 tbsps hot chocolate
crumbled chocolate flake

Method

1. Whip both creams together until they are light and fluffy. Add the sugar, breadcrumbs, coffee and hot chocolate in a bowl and combine well.

2. Place a layer of the breadcrumb mix in the bottom of a serving bowl, followed by a layer of the cream. Repeat the process to the top of the bowl, ending with a cream layer. Refrigerate overnight to set and decorate with crumbled chocolate flake before serving.

Crème Brûlée (Serves 6)

Ingredients

500ml double cream
1/2 vanilla pod, split in 2
6 egg yolks
1 1/2 tbsps caster sugar
Sieved caster sugar, for top

Method

1. Heat the cream slowly in a small pan with the vanilla pod. Just before it boils, remove from the heat, cover and stand for 20 minutes. Then remove the pod and reheat the cream.

2. Beat the eggs in a bowl, add the sugar while beating, then add the hot cream. Stand over a pan of simmering water and stir until it has thickened enough to coat the back of a wooden spoon. Once it reaches this point, remove from the heat and pour into individual ramekin dishes.

3. Bake for 10-12 minutes at 140C/275F/Gas Mark 1, then remove from the oven and leave to cool. Later, make an even layer of sieved caster sugar about 2mm thick over the surface of the dish. Brown under a very hot grill, turning the dish so the sugar browns evenly. Cool again, and chill for several hours, or overnight, before serving.

Lavender Cream (Serves 6)

Ingredients

200g crème fraîche or double cream
1/2 tbsp lavender honey
1/2 tbsp fresh lavender flowers (optional)

Method

1. This delicate cream is delicious served with any chocolate dessert. Put the honey and crème fraîche into a medium bowl and mix together well. Sprinkle lightly with lavender flowers for decoration.

Lemon & Rum Mousse (Serves 4)

Ingredients

110ml/1/2 cup of lemon juice, (strained of pulp)
grated zest of 2 lemons
4 egg yolks
450ml/2 cups of double cream
150g/2/3 cup of sugar
1 sachet of gelatin
4 tbsps white rum
whipped cream (for topping)

Method

1. Place the lemon juice, zest, sugar and egg yolks in a bowl and place over a pan of simmering water. Whisk the ingredients together until thickened. Once thickened, remove from the heat and whip with a hand-blender until cold and dense. Leave to one side.

2. Place the white rum and gelatin in a bowl and leave to one side for 4-5 minutes. Place the bowl over a pan of simmering water and heat until melted. Remove from the heat and leave to cool for 2-3 minutes.

Lemon & Rum Mousse/cont.

3. Place the cream in a bowl and whip with a hand-blender until thick enough to form shapes.

4. Take the gelatin/rum mixture and whisk it into the egg yolk mixture. Then carefully fold in the whipped cream. Transfer the mousse into serving bowls and chill for 20-30 minutes. To serve, top with a little whipped cream, if desired.

Lemon Custard (Serves 3-4)

Ingredients

75ml/1/3 cup of double cream
60ml/1/4 cup of milk
zest of 1/2 lemon (pared)
30g/1/4 cup of caster sugar
1 egg yolk

Method

1. Place the cream, milk and lemon zest into a saucepan and place over a medium heat. Bring to the boil and then immediately remove.

2. Place the egg yolk and sugar in a bowl and beat together. Pour over the boiled milk/cream mixture and mix well. Return to the saucepan and cook over a low heat, stirring continuously, until the custard thickens.

3. Remove from the heat and sieve into a bowl or serving jug. Serve the custard either hot or cold.

Lemon Syllabub (Serves 4)

Ingredients

juice of 1/2 lemon
zest of 1/2 lemon (finely grated)
280ml/1 1/4 cups of double cream
55g/1/4 cup of caster sugar
55ml/1/4 cup of white wine
almond slivers (to garnish)

Method

1. Place the cream and sugar in a bowl and whip together until soft peaks form. Stir in the white wine, lemon juice and 3/4 of the lemon zest.

2. Spoon the dessert into glass serving bowls and sprinkle the top with the remaining zest and some almond slivers.

Ma's Boozy Sherry Trifle (Serves 8-10)

Ingredients for base

175g butter, softened, plus extra for greasing
175g caster sugar
3 eggs, beaten
175g self-raising flour, sifted
225g raspberry jam
150-175ml sweet sherry

Ingredients for custard

5 large eggs
4 tsps caster sugar
1 tsp vanilla extract
750ml milk

Ingredients for topping

400ml double cream
8 glacé cherries
1 chocolate flake bar

Ma's Boozy Sherry Trifle/cont.
Method

1. Heat the oven to 180C/350F/Gas Mark 4. Grease two 20cm sandwich tins and line with greaseproof paper. Beat together the butter and sugar until the mixture looks pale and fluffy. Gradually add in the beaten eggs, beating well between each addition, then fold in the flour.

2. Divide the mixture between the two tins and bake for 20 minutes, or until firm to the touch. Cool in the tins for two minutes, then remove and cool completely on a wire rack. Sandwich the rounds of sponge together with the jam. Set aside.

3. Whisk the eggs with the sugar and vanilla extract. Put the milk in a heavy-bottomed pan and heat until just below boiling, then pour slowly into the egg mix, whisking all the time.

4. Return to the pan and stir over a gentle heat until the custard thickens enough to lightly coat the back of a wooden spoon. Don't let it boil or it will curdle. Leave to cool.

5. Cut the sponge into 2cm chunks. Use half of these to line a large trifle sprinkling generously with sherry as you go. Pour in half the custard and add the remaining sponge. Sprinkle with more sherry, then spread the rest of the custard over the top. Cover and leave for 5-6 hours, or overnight.

6. Whip the cream and spread over the top. Decorate with the cherries and break the flake bar over the top.

Strawberry Rosé Syllabub (Serves 4)
Ingredients

250ml double cream
400g strawberries, sliced
2 tbsp vanilla sugar
100g caster sugar
4 tbsps icing sugar
200ml Sparkling Rosé wine

Method

1. Keeping back 4 small strawberries for decoration, slice the remaining fruit into a bowl. Sprinkle over the vanilla sugar and leave to soak for about 30 minutes, until the sugar has dissolved in the strawberry juice. Place a sheet of non-stick grease proof paper onto a baking tray.

2. Place the caster sugar in a small pan over a medium heat. Do not stir. Watch the sugar until the bottom layer has turned to liquid. Reduce the heat and stir until the sugar has dissolved and is a light caramel colour.

3. Pour onto the sheet of baking parchment and leave to cool and harden. Place a spoonful of the strawberries in the bottom of 4 glasses.

4. Then, using a small food processor or blender, blend the remaining strawberry mixture to a smooth purée. Remove any remaining pips.

5. Pour the cream into a bowl with the icing sugar and sparkling rosé then, using an electric whisk, whisk until the cream forms soft peaks. Using a metal spoon, gently fold in the remaining strawberry purée to create a rippled effect. Spoon this syllabub into the serving glasses. Break the hard caramel into shards and arrange on top of the syllabub. Serve immediately with the reserved strawberries.

Thyme Infused Cream (Serves 4)

Ingredients

142ml carton double cream
2 sprigs fresh thyme
1 tbsp icing sugar

Method

1. Pour the cream into a small pan and add the thyme. Heat gently until just warm, then remove from the heat and leave to cool.

2. Transfer to a bowl, remove the thyme and allow to chill. Whip the cream until it thickens, then sift the icing sugar over the cream and gently fold in. The herby flavour of this cream makes it great with poached soft fruits such as pears or plums.

Almost-Innocent Brownies (Makes 32)

Ingredients

115g/1 cup of flour
100g/1 cup of unsweetened cocoa powder
1 tsp baking powder
225g/1 cup of sugar
2 eggs (lightly beaten)
4 egg whites
225ml/1 cup of unsweetened applesauce
1/4 tsp salt
3 tbsps vegetable oil
4 tsps vanilla extract

Method

1. Preheat the oven to 180C/350F/Gas Mark 4. Spray two 8 x 8in baking trays with low-fat cooking spray.

2. Place the sugar, flour, cocoa powder, salt and baking powder in a bowl and mix together.

3. In a separate bowl, place the applesauce, oil, egg, egg whites and vanilla extract and mix together. Gradually add in the flour mix, stirring in a little at a time until well combined.

4. Pour into the baking trays and place in the oven for 20 minutes. Remove from the oven and leave to cool for 5-10 minutes. Cut each into 16 equal squares.

Per Serving (per brownie): 74kcals, 2.4g Fat.

Baked Pears with Cranberries (Serves 4-5)
Ingredients
3 ripe pears (peeled & quartered)
75g/1/2 cup of dried cranberries
75ml/1/3 cup of pomegranate juice
30g/1/4 cup of walnuts (chopped)

Method
1. Preheat the oven to 180C/350F/Gas Mark 4. Place the pear quarters into a baking dish and pour the pomegranate juice and the cranberries over the top.

2. Place in the oven for 15-20 minutes, until the pears are tender. Serve with low-fat, or fat-free, vanilla yoghurt, if desired.

Per Serving (without yoghurt): 197kcals, 5g Fat.

Carrot Cake (Makes 16 Slices)
Ingredients for cake
115g/1 cup of whole wheat flour
115g/1 cup of flour
4 egg whites
280g/1 1/4 cups of brown sugar
200g/2 cups of shredded carrot
225ml/1 cup of unsweetened applesauce
110ml/1/2 cup of low fat buttermilk
225g/1 cup of canned crushed pineapple (drained)
75g/1/2 cup of raisins
2 tsps bicarbonate of soda
1/4 tsp nutmeg
1/2 tsp allspice
1 tsp vanilla extract

Ingredients icing
250g/2 cups of icing sugar
1/2 tsp vanilla extract
55g/1/4 cup of low-fat cream cheese
1 tsp lemon juice

Method Cake

1. Preheat the oven to 180C/350F/Gas Mark 4. Spray a 13 x 9in baking pan with low-fat cooking spray.

2. Place the bicarbonate of soda, flours and spices in a bowl and stir together well.

3. In a separate bowl, beat the egg whites until soft peaks form. Add in the sugar, little by little and beat well. Follow with the applesauce, vanilla and buttermilk.

4. Add the wet ingredients to the flour mixture and stir in until just moist. Stir in carrots, raisins and pineapple. Spoon the mixture into the baking pan and place in the oven for 35-40 minutes.

5. Remove from the oven and leave to cool for 5-10 minutes. Turn out onto a wire cooling rack to cool completely.

Method Icing

1. Place the cream cheeses, vanilla and lemon juice in a bowl and beat together. Add the icing sugar, stirring it in little by little until reaching a spreading consistency.

2. Spread over the cooled cake and cut into 16 even squares.

Per Serving: 269kcals, 3.3g Fat.

Coffee & Chocolate Mousse (Serves 8)

Ingredients

300ml/1 1/3 cups of half-fat crème fraiche
8 tsps half-fat crème fraiche (to serve)
4 egg whites
2 tbsps coffee essence
4 tsps cocoa powder
2 tsps low-fat drinking chocolate
4 tsps powdered gelatine
4 tbsps boiling water
4 tbsps caster sugar

Coffee & Chocolate Mousse/cont.

Method

1. Place the coffee essence in a bowl. In another bowl, mix together the cocoa powder and drinking chocolate.

2. Divide the crème fraiche equally between both bowls and mix well. Place the gelatine in a bowl with the boiling water to dissolve. Place the bowl to one side.

3. Place the sugar and egg whites in a bowl and whisk until stiff. Divide this mixture between the coffee and chocolate bowls and mix in well. Divide the gelatine between the two bowls and fold in carefully using a metal spoon.

4. Alternate a spoonful of each of the mixtures into dessert glasses, until about 3/4 full and swirl together gently. Place in the refrigerator for 1 hour. When ready to serve, top each with a teaspoon of crème fraiche and dust over lightly with cocoa powder.

Per Serving: 130kcals, 6.5g Fat.

Fruit Muffins (Makes 20)
Ingredients
460g/4 cups of self-raising wholemeal flour
2 eggs (beaten)
620ml/2 3/4 cups of skimmed milk
3 tsps baking powder
55ml/1/2 cup of light muscovado sugar
150g/2/3 cup of dried apricots (finely chopped)
25g/ 1/4 cup of raisins
2 bananas (mashed)
2 tbsps orange juice
3 tbsps corn oil
2 tsps orange rind (finely grated)
4 tbsps porridge oats

Method
1. Preheat the oven to 200C/400F/Gas Mark 6. Line 2 cupcake baking trays with 20 paper muffin cases.

2. Sift the baking powder and flour into a large bowl and stir in the sugar, raisins and chopped apricots.

3. Make a well in the centre of the ingredients and add the milk, eggs, banana, oil and orange rind. Mix together well.

4. Spoon the mixture into the muffin liners, up to about 3/4 full. Sprinkle over the top with the porridge oats.

5. Place in the centre of oven for 30 minutes, until risen and firm to touch.

6. Remove from the oven and leave to cool for 5 minutes. Remove the cupcakes from the baking tray and place on a wire rack to cool.

Per Serving: 180kcals, 1.5g Fat.

Red Berry Salad with Frothy Sauce (Serves 4)

Ingredients for salad

200g/1 cup of strawberries (halved)
100g/1 cup of redcurrants (trimmed)
100g/1 cup of cranberries
225ml/1 cup of unsweetened apple juice
150g/2/3 cup of light muscovado sugar
1 cinnamon stick (broken)

Ingredients for sauce

1/2 cup of marshmallows
125g/1 cup of raspberries
2 tbsps blackcurrant cordial

Method for salad

1. Place the sugar, cranberries, redcurrants, apple juice and cinnamon stick in a saucepan and place over a medium/high heat. Bring to the boil, then reduce the heat and simmer for 8-10 minutes.

2. Add in the strawberries and stir well. Once mixed, remove from the heat and transfer the mixture to a large bowl. Cover and leave to cool for 10 minutes, before transferring the bowl into the refrigerator for 1 hour. On removing the bowl from the refrigerator, discard the cinnamon stick.

Method for sauce

1. Place the blackcurrant cordial and raspberries in a saucepan and place over a medium/high heat. Bring to the boil, then reduce the heat and simmer for 3 minutes, until the fruit begins to soften.

2. Add in the marshmallows and heat through, stirring continuously, until the marshmallows melt.

3. Transfer the berry salad into serving bowls and spoon over the warm sauce. Serve immediately.

Per Serving: 220kcals, 0.3g Fat.

Summer Fruit Brûlée (Serves 8)
Ingredients
900ml/4 cups of summer fruits (strawberries, redcurrants, raspberries, etc)
300ml/1 1/3 cups of low-fat natural yoghurt
300ml/1 1/3 cups of soured cream
8 tbsps demerara sugar
2 tsps vanilla extract

Method
1. Equally divide the summer fruits between 8 heatproof ramekin dishes. Place the fromage frais, soured cream and vanilla extract in a bowl and mix together well. Spoon the mixture over the fruit, covering the fruit completely.

2. Top each with a serving of 1 tablespoon of demerara sugar and place under a hot grill for 3-4 minutes, until the sugar begins to caramelise. Remove from the grill and leave to cool for 2 minutes before serving.

Per Serving: 165kcals, 7g Fat.

Summer Fruit Salad (Serves 6)
Ingredients
100g/1/2 cup of strawberries (halved)
50g/1/2 cup of blueberries
60g/1/2 cup of raspberries
50g/1/2 cup of blackberries
100g/1 cup of redcurrants
150g/3/4 cup of caster sugar
6 tbsps low-fat fromage frais
5 tbsps water
grated rind of 1 orange
juice of 1 orange
2 tsps arrowroot
2 tbsps port

Method
1. Place the water, grated orange rind and sugar in a saucepan and heat over a medium heat, stirring continuously until the sugar has dissolved.

Summer Fruit Salad/cont.

2. Add the orange juice and redcurrants and bring to the boil. Reduce the heat and simmer for 2-3 minutes. Remove from the heat and drain, reserve the syrup and place the redcurrants in a bowl. Place the arrowroot in a bowl and mix with a little water.

3. Return the reserved syrup to the saucepan and add in the arrowroot. Bring to the boil, stirring continuously until the mixture thickens. Stir in the port, mixing it in well.

4. Pour the syrup over the redcurrants in the bowl and add in the rest of the summer fruits. Mix the fruits together well and leave to cool. Once cooled, serve in dessert dishes with a tablespoon of the low-fat fromage frais.

Per Serving: 110kcals, 0.1g Fat.

Tangy Fruit Fool (Serves 8)
Ingredients
845ml/3 3/4 cups of low-fat custard
4 egg whites
2 ripe mangoes (peeled & chopped)
3 passion fruit
4 kiwi fruit (peeled & chopped)
2 bananas (chopped)
4 tbsps lime juice
1 tsp lime rind (finely grated)
1 tsp vanilla extract

Method

1. Place the chopped mango in a food processor and blend until smooth. Place the chopped kiwi and banana into a bowl and add in the lime juice and grated rind. Mix together well.

2. Place the egg whites in a bowl and whisk until stiff. Gently fold in the custard and vanilla extract. In 8 tall dessert glasses, place a layer of chopped fruit, then the mango puree, followed by the custard mixture.

3. Repeat this layering, finishing at the top with the custard mixture. Place in the refrigerator for 30 minutes. Halve the passion fruits and scoop out the seeds. Spoon the fruit over the chilled 'fools' and serve.

Per Serving: 170kcals, 0.6g Fat.

Very-Berry Sorbet (Serves 8)

Ingredients

400g/2 cups of strawberries
125g/1 cup of raspberries
100g/1 cup of blueberries
110g/1/2 cup of sugar
110ml/1/2 cup of water

Method

1. Place all the ingredients in a blender and blend on high until smooth. Pour the mixture through a sieve into a freezer-safe container.

2. Place in the refrigerator to freeze for about 2-3 hours. Remove from the freezer about 10 minutes before serving to soften a little.

Per Serving: 83kcals, 3g Fat.

Zabaglione (Serves 8)

Ingredients

400g/1 3/4 cups of caster sugar

300ml/1 1/3 cups of sweet sherry

10 egg yolks

Method

1. Place the egg yolks in a bowl and add the sugar. Whisk together until the mixture is pale and thick.

2. Place the bowl over a saucepan of boiling water and add the sweet sherry, continuously whisking until the mixture becomes light, frothy and warm.

3. Pour the mixture into 8 dessert glasses. Serve with amaretti biscuits or fresh fruit, if desired.

Per Serving: 158kcals, 1g Fat.

INDEX

A

Allspice & Chocolate Slices, pp 63

Almond & Apricot Tart, pp 21

Almond Tartlets with Raspberry Jam, pp 21

Almost-Innocent Brownies, pp 83

Apple & Blackberry Fruit Dessert, pp 51

Apple & Blackberry Pie, pp 22

Apple & Currant Pastries, pp 23

Apple & Brandy Ice Cream Shells, pp 39

Apple & Mixed Berry Compote, pp 52

Apple & Strawberry Crumble, pp 23

Apple Pie, pp 5

Apple Turnover Tart, pp 6

Apricots with Honey Yoghurt, pp 52

B

Baked Apples, pp 7

Baked Pears with Cranberries, pp 84

Bakewell Tart, pp 7

Baklavas, pp 8

Banana & Berry Delight with Nutmeg, pp 53

Banana Splits, pp 40

Berry Ripple, pp 53

Blueberry & Plum Pie, pp 24

Blueberry Tart, pp 25

Bread & Butter Pudding, pp 9

Buttermilk Vanilla Ice Cream, pp 40

C

Carrot Cake, pp 84

Chantilly Meringues, pp 75

Cherry & Almond Spice Slices, pp 54

Cherry Pie, pp 10

Cherry Tartlets, pp 27

Cheesecake Crumble, pp 26

Chocolate & Banana Mighty Mousse, pp 63

Chocolate & Coffee Dessert Pots, pp 64

Coffee & Chocolate Mousse, pp 85

Chocolate & Orange Tartlets, pp 64

Chocolate Cream Dream, pp 76

Chocolate-Dream Dessert, pp 66

Chocolate Fondue & Fruit, pp 66

Chocolate Fudge Liqueur Sauce, pp 67

Chocolate Ice Cream Cake, pp 67

Chocolate Mint Ice Cream, pp 41

Chocolate Mousse, pp 68

Chocolate Pudding, pp 11

Chocolate Pudding Melt, pp 69

Chocolate Raisin & Liqueur Ice Cream, pp 42

Chocolate Slices, pp 70

Cinnamon & Chilli Chocolate Fondue, pp 71

Citrus Meringues, pp 55

93

T

V

W

Z

Spoons to millilitres

1/2 teaspoon	2.5 ml	1 Tablespoon	15 ml
1 teaspoon	5 ml	2 Tablespoons	30 ml
1-1 1/2 teaspoons	7.5 ml	3 Tablespoons	45 ml
2 teaspoons	10 ml	4 Tablespoons	60 ml

Grams to ounces

10g	0.25oz	225g	8oz
15g	0.38oz	250g	9oz
25g	1oz	275g	10oz
50g	2oz	300g	11oz
75g	3oz	350g	12oz
110g	4oz	375g	13oz
150g	5oz	400g	14oz
175g	6oz	425g	15oz
200g	7oz	450g	16oz

Metric to cups

Description			
Flour etc	115g	1 cup
Clear honey etc	350g	1 cup
Liquids etc	225ml	1 cup

Liquid measures

5fl oz	1/4 pint	150 ml
7.5fl oz		215 ml
10fl oz	1/2 pint	275 ml
15fl oz		425 ml
20fl oz	1 pint	570 ml
35fl oz		1 litre

Oven Temperatures

Gas mark	°F	°C
1	275°F	140°C
2	300°F	150°C
3	325°F	170°C
4	350°F	180°C
5	375°F	190°C
6	400°F	200°C
7	425°F	220°C
8	450°F	230°C
9	475°F	240°C

The recipes contained in this book are passed on in good faith but the publisher cannot be held responsible for any adverse results. Please be aware that certain recipes may contain nuts. The recipes use both metric and imperial measurements, and the reader should not mix metric and imperial measurements. Spoon measurements are level, teaspoons are assumed to be 5ml, tablespoons 15ml. Times given are for guidance only, as preparation techniques may vary and can lead to different cooking times.